GLOBETROTTER™

Trav

HONG
KONG

HELEN OON

NEW
HOLLAND

NEW
HOLLAND

★★★ Highly recommended
★★ Recommended
★ See if you can

First edition published in 2009
by New Holland Publishers (UK) Ltd
London • Cape Town • Sydney • Auckland
10 9 8 7 6 5 4 3 2 1

website: www.newhollandpublishers.com

Garfield House, 86 Edgware Road
London W2 2EA
United Kingdom

80 McKenzie Street
Cape Town 8001
South Africa

Unit 1, 66 Gibbes Street,
Chatswood, NSW 2067
Australia

218 Lake Road
Northcote, Auckland
New Zealand

Distributed in the USA by
The Globe Pequot Press
Connecticut

Publishing Manager: Thea Grobbelaar
DTP Cartographic Manager: Genené Hart
Editor: Thea Grobbelaar
Design and DTP: Nicole Bannister
Cartographer: Reneé Spocter
Picture Researcher: Felicia Apollis
Consultant: Polly Evans
Proofreader: Carla Zietsman
Reproduction by Resolution, Cape Town
Printed and bound by Times Offset (M) Sdn. Bhd., Malaysia

Photographic Credits:
Compliments of **Hong Kong Disneyland®:** pages 97, 98;
Compliments of **The Peninsula Hong Kong Hotel:** page 13;
Nigel Hicks: pages 52, 58, 64, 85;
Helen Oon: pages 8, 10, 15, 32, 39, 44, 57, 60, 63, 79, 81, 82, 89, 90, 94, 101, 104, 106, 111;
Imagebroker/Photo Access: page 86;
SIME/Photo Access: page 35;
Pictures Colour Library: title page, pages 4, 12, 17, 22, 25, 29, 30, 36, 62, 115, 119, 120;
Jane Sweeney/awl-images.com: cover;
Travel Pix Collection/awl-images.com: pages 19, 21, 40, 42, 72, 77, 108.

Copyright © 2009 in text: Helen Oon
Copyright © 2009 in maps: Globetrotter Travel Maps
Copyright © 2009 in photographs:
Individual photographers as credited (right)
Copyright © 2009 New Holland Publishers (UK) Ltd

Acknowledgments:
The author and publishers would like to thank the follow-ing for their help in preparing this guide: The Peninsula Hong Kong, Holiday Inn Golden Mile Hong Kong and The Mira Hong Kong, as well as Travel Asia (HK) Ltd and Splendid Tours.

ISBN 978 1 84773 476 1

Keep us Current
Information in travel guides is apt to change, which is why we regularly update our guides. We'd be grateful to receive feedback if you've noted something we should include in our updates. If you have new information, please share it with us by writing to the Publishing Manager, Globetrotter, at the office nearest to you (addresses on this page). The most significant contribution to each new edition will receive a free copy of the updated guide.

This guidebook has been written by independent authors and updaters. The information therein represents their impartial opinion, and neither they nor the publishers accept payment in return for including in the book or writing more favourable reviews of any of the establish-ments. Whilst every effort has been made to ensure that this guidebook is accurate and up to date as possible, please be aware that the facts quoted are subject to change, particularly the price of food, transport and accommodation. The Publisher accepts no responsibility or liability for any loss, injury or inconvenience incurred by readers or travellers using this guide.

Cover: *One of several Buddha statues, Ngong Ping.*
Title Page: *Skyline and Chinese junk viewed from Kowloon.*

CONTENTS

1
Introducing
Hong Kong

When Hong Kong Island (the 'Fragrant Harbour') and the Kowloon Peninsula (the 'Nine Dragons') became one political region, it was a marriage made in heaven. The Chinese believe that this auspicious combination enjoys excellent feng shui, the ancient Chinese philosophy of environmental management (*see* panel, page 9). Hong Kong is blessed with natural beauty – mountains, valleys, beaches, unspoilt outlying islands – and a sheltered natural harbour that brings phenomenal success to the city as a major shipping hub. The buildings that line Victoria Harbour dazzle with steel and glass, and at night are lit with extravagant neon. Hong Kong may be small in size but its attractions are legion and its importance as one of the world's leading industrial and financial centres is renowned.

Dubbed as Asia's World City, Hong Kong is a living and thriving culture of East-meets-West through its legacy as a British colony for over 150 years and its ancestral roots in China. While it embraces modernity and Western culture wholeheartedly, it is also steeped in Chinese traditions and values. From the high-flying corporate executives and powerful tycoons to the rural villagers, respect for their ancestral beliefs is deep-rooted. Temples and shrines are everywhere, even in the busiest commercial districts of Kowloon and Hong Kong Island.

The uninitiated may be forgiven for thinking that Hong Kong is nothing more than a cityscape dominated by skyscrapers because its reputation as a city is very much that. But a visitor will be pleasantly surprised by

TOP ATTRACTIONS

*** **Victoria Harbour:** great architecture, harbour cruise, nightly Symphony of Lights.
*** **The Peak:** spectacular 360-degree panoramic view, iconic Peak Tram ride.
*** **historical quarters** in Central, colonial architecture.
*** **Ocean Park:** aquatic park with giant pandas.
*** **Hong Kong Disneyland®:** Disney magic for family fun.
*** **Ngong Ping Village/ cable car ride:** cultural village, view of Lantau Island.
*** **Tian Tan:** world's biggest outdoor seated Buddha.
** **Lamma Island:** untouched by urban development.

Opposite: *The iconic skyline of the harbour front.*

the many hidden attractions of Hong Kong beyond the shadows of the skyscrapers. While the main attractions in Kowloon and Hong Kong – great shopping, a wide choice of accommodation, superb dining experiences and scenic harbour cruises – are not to be missed, the countryside in the New Territories and the outlying islands are worth exploring. With its sophisticated and efficient transport system, these destinations are easily accessible and fares are inexpensive.

With such a fascinating and diverse lineage, Hong Kong is an exciting, extraordinary destination, excellent for exploring the mysteries of the East and the very best of Chinese culture and customs. It deserves to be more than just a brief stopover destination between east and west. Boasting an impressive tourist arrival of over 28 million (2007 figure), its tag line 'Hong Kong – Live It. Love It!' lives up to its promise.

THE LAND

Hong Kong is abutted by the Guangdong Province in China on its northern border and surrounded by the South China Sea on its eastern, western and southern shores. With a landmass of more than 1104km² (426 sq miles), Hong Kong has four main regions: **Hong Kong Island**, a hilly island in the Pearl River Delta, which lends its name to the region; **Kowloon**, a peninsula on the mainland on the opposite side of the delta, flanked by the **New Territories** in the north; and 260 outlying **islands**, mostly uninhabited. **Lantau**, the biggest of these, is twice the size of Hong Kong Island and is the site of **Hong Kong Disneyland**® and the new **Hong Kong International Airport** (HKIA) at Chek Lap Kok, which opened in 1998. The channel between Kowloon and Hong Kong Island forms an excellent deepwater harbour that has secured Hong Kong its position as an important entrepôt on a major international shipping route since the 19th century.

Hong Kong's **topography** and **geology** are defined by rugged terrain furrowed by steep spurs and valleys. **Tai Mo Shan**, in the New Territories, is the highest peak, rising to 957m (3140ft), while on Hong Kong Island the **Victoria Peak**, at 552m (1811ft) high, offers a panorama of Victoria Harbour and Kowloon and is one of Hong Kong's top tourist attractions. The mountains are mainly volcanic rock, while the lowlands are generally granite and sedimentary rock. The Chinese believe the mountain ranges represent dragons (see panel, page 9).

On Hong Kong Island, the rugged coasts are interspersed with scenic enclaves of sandy **beaches** such as in **Repulse Bay** and **Stanley Peninsula**, two of Hong Kong's most popular beaches for the locals and tourists. The remote coasts around the **Sai Kung Peninsula** in the New Territories feature unspoilt pristine beaches.

The spectacular mountainous landscape and wild natural beauty in the New Territories, Lantau Island and Lamma Island offer great trails for the popular pastimes of **hiking** and **hill climbing**. Visitors to Hong Kong are often pleasantly surprised by the vibrant outdoor adventures available away from the concrete jungle of the city.

FACT FILE

Geographical location: Pearl River Delta, adjacent to Guangdong Province in southern China.
Territories: Hong Kong Island, Kowloon Peninsula, New Territories and 260 outlying islands.
Population: 6.92 million (2007), of which 95 per cent are Chinese.
Largest group of foreign nationals: Filipinos (133,100, mostly domestic workers).
Overall density: 6410 people per sq km.
Housing: About 2.1 million people live in 715,700 public rental high-rise housing estates of the Hong Kong Housing Authority and the Hong Kong Housing Society.
Area: 1104km² (426 sq miles).
Climate: Subtropical.
Religion: Buddhism and Taoism are the main religions. Others are Christianity, Islam, Hinduism, Sikhism and Judaism.
Official Languages: Cantonese, Mandarin and English.
National emblem: Bauhinia.
National Motto: 'Can-do' spirit.

Above: *The tram is a historical mode of transport on Hong Kong Island, offering an enjoyable and economical way to see the sights.*

Climate

Due to its geographical position, Hong Kong enjoys a **subtropical** climate. January and February tend to have gloomy skies, with occasional cold fronts influenced by the cold northerly winds, and temperatures can drop below 10°C (50°F). By March and April, the weather gets milder but humid, while in May to August the temperature rises considerably, often exceeding 30°C (86°F), with high humidity. Between June and October, the region is subjected to typhoons bringing in high winds and torrential rain, sometimes causing landslides and flooding. Hong Kong has an official typhoon warning system ranging in ascending order of gale force 1 to 10 in order of severity, with 1 being just a standby warning, rising to 10 when people are advised to stay indoors, batten down the hatches and be prepared for the worst. Up-to-date information indicating the strength of the impending gale force can be obtained from radio and television broadcasts or display boards at shopping malls and other strategic positions in the city. You can also find weather information on www.weather. gov.hk In the past, warnings were given in the form of firing a typhoon gun and later exploding a bomb, but due to the heavy traffic noise and the increase in the number of high-rise buildings, this system became ineffective and it was abolished. Visitors should not be unduly worried as long as they heed the warnings and follow the official instructions.

HISTORY IN BRIEF

Hong Kong started life as a small fishing village on an infertile rocky island surrounded by pirate-infested waters. During the Qing Dynasty, at the end of the 18th century, the British dominated the foreign trade in Canton (present-day Guangzhou). There were tensions between the Chinese and British due to the vast disparity in culture and what the British deemed unfavourable trading terms and conditions. Britain had used Hong Kong Island as a transit stop for refuelling and rest, and reportedly often colluded with the pirates, especially in the trading of illegal opium from British India. The Chinese's attempt to stamp out the opium trade led to a war known as the **Opium War** (1839–41). The war started when the Chinese government confiscated opium warehouses in Canton owned by British merchants. The British retaliated by sending an expedition of warships to the city, and their superior weaponry won them a quick victory.

The British decided the settlement for a Sino-British commercial relation was more advantageous. An agreement was reached with the signing of the **Convention of Chuenpi** on 20 January 1841. The British flag was hoisted at Possession Point in the vicinity of present-day Hollywood Road Park in Sheung Wan in the district of Central on 26 January 1841 and the British formally took possession of the island in June of the same year. Thus the seed was sown for the birth of the modern history of Hong Kong. But the incumbent British Foreign Secretary at the time, **Lord Palmerston**, was not impressed with the island and contemptuously dismissed it as a 'barren island with hardly a house upon it'. He demanded an alternative trade treaty and a year later the **Nanking Treaty** was signed. Under the treaty, signed in 1842, China was forced to pay a large indemnity and to open up five ports, including Canton, to the British for both trade and residence. In addition, the British demanded an island for settlement where they could live and trade under their own protectorate.

Tensions were still brewing between the two nations and neither side was happy with the terms of the Convention. The cession of a part of China to a foreign country had made the Chinese 'lose face', and anger and resentment set in. Things came to a head when Canton police boarded the British ship *Arrow* in search of suspected pirates and then charged its crew with smuggling. The British seized this opportunity to demand more trading rights by launching another offensive against the Chinese, this time assisted by the French. The war, known as the **Anglo-Chinese War** or **Second Opium War**, was a swift victory for the

FENG SHUI AND LAND OF NINE DRAGONS

The ancient philosophy of feng shui (meaning 'wind-water') has been practised in China by emperors and the common people for five millennia. It is based on harnessing and maximizing the energy of the earth to create a congenial living and working environment. Mountains, wind and water play a pivotal role in influencing earth's energy and the practice of feng shui aims to direct this energy into buildings and their surrounds and to deflect any negative 'vibes'. The Chinese often refer to mountains as 'dragon ranges', which shelter and support buildings. The dragon is considered to be the most auspicious and powerful celestial animal in Chinese culture and is the emblem of the emperors. Legend has it that when a boy emperor from the Sung Dynasty fled the warring states across the border, he counted eight mountain ranges in the landscape and he called the land 'Eight Dragons'. His servant reminded him that since he was the emperor, he was also a dragon. So he named the region 'Kowloon', meaning 'Nine Dragons'. The Chinese believe the eight 'dragon' ranges in the north and the water in the harbour front have the most auspicious feng shui, which brings wealth and prosperity to the region. Today feng shui is an intrinsic part of Hong Kong society.

British-French alliance in 1858. This resulted in the British securing the Kowloon Peninsula and later Kowloon City and the New Territories, which were leased for 99 years from 1898.

The island, dismissed as a 'worthless piece of rock' by the British Parliament in 1841, was soon to be their cash cow. Its strategic geographical location, enhanced by a natural harbour, commanded the trade routes of the Far East and the colony grew rapidly into a thriving entrepôt with banks, factories, warehouses and ship-yards springing up as its reputation as a trading post spread. The British operated a two-tiered system, creating excellent infrastructure, schools, hospitals and fine buildings for themselves and their workforce, but scant improvement for the majority of the local residents who had grown in great numbers with the influx of migrants from China. However, Hong Kong became a centre for missionary work and there were educational opportunities for young Chinese. It was also a refuge for those opposing the Chinese Republican and Communist government, notably **Sun Yat Sen**, the Father of Modern China, who fled to Hong Kong after a failed uprising (*see* the Dr Sun Yat Sen Museum, page 26).

In December 1941, Japan invaded Hong Kong after defeating the British. The occupation lasted three years and eight months. The British became prisoners of war and the population was brutalized and suffered extreme hardship, with the economy grinding to a halt and public services seriously disrupted. The Japanese surrendered in August 1945 and the British resumed power. After many post-war trials and tribulations, Hong Kong once again emerged as a world-class economic powerhouse, branching out

Below: *Dr Sun Yat Sen, known as the 'Father of Modern China', is immortalized in bronze; this statue, standing proudly in front of the Dr Sun Yat Sen Museum, portrays him in his youth, dressed in a traditional Chinese costume.*

into industries and manufacturing. Today it is the envy of the world as an economic success story – the 'Nine Dragons of the East'.

On 1 July 1997, as the British and Hong Kong flags were lowered and the Chinese national and Hong Kong Special Administrative Region (HKSAR) flags were raised to replace them, the handover of Hong Kong to mainland China was celebrated with much pomp and ceremony (at least by the Chinese). China declared that Hong Kong would be governed under a 'One Country, Two Systems' policy that would allow the people to maintain their social and economic status for the next 50 years from the date of the handover, as agreed by the Sino-British Joint Declaration.

GOVERNMENT AND ECONOMY

Effective 1 July 1997, Hong Kong officially became the **Hong Kong Special Administrative Region** (HKSAR) of the People's Republic of China (PRC) and the **Basic Law** came into force on the same day. Under the Basic Law, the HKSAR will keep its capitalist system, will have freedom of speech and religion, and will enjoy a high degree of political and economic autonomy in accordance with the principle of 'One Country, Two Systems', maintaining executive, legislative and independent judicial power, including that of final adjudication, for the next 50 years. The executive authorities and legislature of HKSAR consist entirely of Hong Kong permanent residents, headed by the Chief

Above: *The financial district in Central boasts of many landmark buildings, including the architecturally fascinating Bank of China in the background.*
Opposite: *The Peninsula Hong Kong in Kowloon is synonymous with classic style and elegant old-world charm; it is famed for its fleet of Rolls Royces.*

Executive, aided by the Executive Council and supported by the Legislative Council, to set in place the Basic Law. The law requires that the region continues to operate a capitalist economic and trade system and remains a free port, a separate customs territory and an international financial centre. In addition, HKSAR can maintain and develop its own foreign policy when dealing with other countries and international organizations in relation to economic, trade, financial and monetary matters, as well as shipping, communications, tourism, culture and sport, officiating under the name 'Hong Kong, China'. In other words, the political power might have changed hands but to the outsider little seems to have changed and the Motherland has welcomed Hong Kong back like a parent would welcome a very successful son who has gone overseas and prospered and is now back to join the family firm.

The Dragon of Asia

Hong Kong's prowess as one of the most important economic powerhouses in the world is largely due to its **human resources**. It is blessed with a diligent, adaptable, well-educated and skilled workforce with a 'can-do' attitude. The people's entrepreneurial and industrious characteristics have contributed to its robust economic growth and helped to establish its position as 'the 11th largest trading economy, the sixth largest foreign exchange market and the 15th largest banking centre in the world', according to HKSAR Government Information Services Department. It practises a market-led economy, a free-trade and free-market policy with no trade barriers, no discrimination against overseas investors, freedom of capital movement and well-established and comprehensive financial networks. In addition, it has an excellent transport and communications infrastructure, impartial rule of law, transparent regulations and low and predictable taxation. Its close integration with mainland China has opened up a vast production hinterland and market outlet for Hong Kong manufacturers. To date, Hong Kong is one of the largest trading partners of China.

Hong Kong is also one of the world's leading exporters of garments, watches and clocks, toys, games and electronic products. Its strategic geographical location and gateway to China make it one of the world's busiest container ports and busiest airports in terms of number of passengers and volume of cargo handled.

Tourism

Tourism plays a major part in the economy of Hong Kong and the **Tourism Commission**, a government body, does a lot to make the country user-friendly for tourists by upgrading and enhancing tourist infrastructure, attractions and facilities. The country saw its tourist numbers increase by 11.6 per cent in 2007, with a record high of 28.17 million arrivals including a large percentage from mainland China. With this boom in tourism, the average hotel occupancy is about 86 per cent throughout the year and there are hotels to suit every budget. The Victoria Peak, Ocean Park, Hong Kong Disneyland®, Hong Kong Wetland, Ngong Ping Village, Po Lin Monastery/Giant Buddha and other major attractions are constantly being improved to maintain a high standard for tourists. Signage to popular tourist spots has been enhanced with easy-to-follow directional signs, map and identification boards with useful information about the sites to guide visitors. Hong Kong's public transport is

HONG KONG MOBILE HOST

This service is ideal for independent visitors who prefer to do DIY tours. Using your own mobile phone, you can access audio information on tourist attractions, shopping, dining, entertainment, weather forecast and current events. The service is available in English, Putonghua (Standard Mandarin) and Cantonese. There are three options: purchase a three-day unlimited **Mobile Host PIN Card** (roaming charges waived) for HK$60; use an **international roaming** service (roaming charges apply), or use a **Pay As You Go** service by dialling *454, selecting language and accessing the Main Menu. The Mobile Host PIN Card can be purchased at shops displaying the Hong Kong Mobile Host sign, at HKTB Visitor Information and Service centres, or at selected retail shops of participating mobile network operations (www.discover hongkong.com/mobile).

among the best in the world, with an efficient, comfortable and comprehensive network. Hong Kong's liberal visa policy for visitors, including visa-free visits for people staying from seven to 180 days, is applicable to 170 countries. To facilitate its promotion and marketing worldwide, the **Hong Kong Tourism Board** was set up in major cities around the world. It is no wonder that Hong Kong has become a mecca for visitors worldwide.

THE PEOPLE

Initially, the social and economic climate was not very healthy under the British rule. Population numbers rose dramatically. Crime was rife and disease and typhoons threatened lives and properties. The 1948–49 civil war in China between the Chinese Nationalist Government and the Communists led to a huge exodus of people from Kwangtung Province (present-day Guangdong), Shanghai and other commercial centres, all flocking to Hong Kong. Although wary of foreign rule, the ever-pragmatic migrants thrived under a liberal British rule. The success of Hong Kong was built on the human spirit – people were willing and eager to work hard and prosper.

Today, out of a population of nearly 7 million people, 95% are **Chinese**. Hong Kong's open-door policy, complemented with a vibrant and stable economy, attracts people from all over the world to invest and work in a dynamic environment. It welcomes people with skill, knowledge and experience to contribute and add value to the economy.

As the country becomes more affluent and the standard of living rises among the professionals, the demand for domestic workers increases. Today, the largest number of migrant workers come from the **Philippines**, mostly employed as domestic helpers, although **Thai** and **Indonesian** workers are now on the increase. Every Sunday it is customary for the foreign domestic workers on their day off to gather in huge numbers in parks (and even under traffic flyovers in inclement weather) to socialize with their fellow country people. There are picnics and music, creating quite a carnival atmosphere, albeit within their own social group. It is quite a unique phenomenon in Hong Kong.

Religion and Festivals

Under the government's Basic Law, there is religious freedom for all citizens and residents of Hong Kong. With such a cosmopolitan society, all the **main religions** – Buddhism, Taoism, Confucianism, Christianity, Islam, Hinduism, Sikhism and Judaism – are practised here.

Underneath the façade of a thoroughly modern society, the Chinese are deeply entrenched in their **traditional worship** and beliefs, judging by the abundance of temples and monasteries throughout the country. Many still seek the advice of fortune-tellers for engagements, weddings and prediction charts of their personal lives. Feng shui masters are frequently consulted for important matters such as the orientation and design of houses and offices, auspicious times and dates to move house or relocate an office, and advice on placements of objects in interior decoration.

Above: *A Buddhist monk at prayer in front of an altar in a Buddhist monastery; the altar, ornately decorated with religious artefacts, is laden with votive offerings for the three golden statues of Buddha.*

Buddhism and Taoism are the dominant religions, as befit a Chinese country. The plethora of **religious festivals** are celebrated with much fervour and lively pageantry accompanied by a visual feast of colours and sound. A festival is a wonderful way of gaining an insight into the soul of the Chinese culture. Festival dates are not fixed as they are based on the lunar calendar and therefore dependent on the cycles of the moon. The principal and most spectacular festivals are Chinese New Year, Mid-Autumn Festival and Dragon Boat Festival.

Buddhism plays a major role among the population and the main festival they celebrate is **Buddha's birthday** that takes place on the eighth day of the fourth month in the lunar calendar (May). The festival is celebrated with prayer sessions throughout the day and bathing of the statues of Buddha. Thousands of devotees flock to major temples and monasteries throughout the country to pay respect to Sakyamuni Buddha, Kwan Yin – the Goddess of Mercy – and other deities. Tian Tan Giant Buddha at Po Lin Monastery on Lantau Island is the centre of the celebration.

Taoism also has a large following and its festivals are legion. Taoists worship a vast pantheon of gods and patron saints, mostly based on mortals who have great virtues and who have played an important part in the wellbeing of mankind. Among the immortal gods, **Tin Hau** – the Queen of Heaven and Protector of Seafarers – is the most revered in this seafaring nation. Her birthday is celebrated on the 23rd day of the third month of the lunar calendar (April), especially among fishermen and seafaring communities. Boats are decked out in colourful flags and ribbons and offerings are made to thank the goddess for her protection and also for their future safety, that they be blessed with an abundant sea harvest and safe sea journeys. The celebration culminates in a lively procession with vividly coloured paper prayer offerings on floats parading on the street to the various Tin Hau temples.

Chinese New Year

The most important festival in the Chinese calendar is Chinese New Year, popularly known as the **Spring Festival** or the **Lunar New Year**, celebrated on the first new moon of the year, usually in January or February, and lasting for 15 days. Preparation starts a month in advance with a thorough spring cleaning of the home to ward off bad luck from the old year, stocking up enough food for a feast, and buying new clothes and decorations for the house. The celebration starts with a family reunion dinner on New Year's Eve, feasting on auspicious food such as fish for prosperity, chicken and pork to bring abundance, and other festive delicacies. On New Year's Day, friends and relatives have open-house celebrations when they visit one another's homes bringing gifts, usually Mandarin oranges to represent gifts of gold, as the word for 'orange' is very similar to the word for 'gold' in Cantonese. The festival ends with the **Yuen Siu** or **Spring Lantern Festival** on the 15th day to celebrate the first full moon of the Chinese New Year, with colourful lanterns in traditional designs festooned

all over parks, restaurants and homes. Another big feast is held among families to end the celebration. Spectacular lantern processions parade around town, traditionally to guide roving spirits of the dead back to the nether world, but in modern Hong Kong it is more a carnival of light and romance. Love is in the air as this festival is equivalent to St Valentine's Day in the Western culture. Lovers pledge their love for one another under the moonlight and glowing lanterns. Traditionally, single ladies will wish upon the moon for their future husbands by throwing oranges into the sea or river as spiritual offerings.

Above: *The Chinese dragon dance plays an important part in major Chinese festivals.*

Mid-Autumn Festival

This important festival is also known as the **Moon Cake Festival** and usually takes place in September or October, determined by the lunar calendar. This is the season for farmers to mark the end of the summer harvest. During the autumn equinox, the harvest moon is at its full glory and is celebrated with lavish lantern displays in parks and on the streets. **Victoria Park** is the main venue for the lantern extravaganza, with the locals gathering to adore the large full moon and feast on moon cakes. These round pastries are filled with a sweet paste of lotus seeds, sesame seeds or red beans, some embellished with hard-boiled salted egg yolks.

MOON JADE RABBIT

Chinese culture abounds with legend and mythology. It is believed that during the harvest full moon you can see the shape of a rabbit and a lady. It was said that a rabbit had pleased the gods with its selflessness on earth, was rewarded and sent to live in the Moon Palace and became known as the Jade Rabbit. He can be seen pounding the herbs of elixir of immortality for the gods with Chang Er, the immortal lady of the moon. In some Chinese beliefs, it is disrespectful to point at the moon as it might offend the immortals who will inflict an ear infection on the offending mortal for not listening to their words of advice.

Aside from shark's fins, the most expensive ingredient in Chinese *haute cuisine* is bird's nest. This pricey delicacy is the nests of white-nest swiftlets (*Aerodramus fuciphagus*) and black-nest swiftlets (*Aerodramus maximus*), mostly found in Southeast Asia, notably in Niah and Gomantung caves in Borneo. The white nests are considered more superior and purer in quality and can fetch up to US$10,000 per kilogram. The birds roost in caves; they make nests on the cave ceilings from their slimy gum-like saliva which hardens into boat-shaped nests. The natives of Borneo often risk their lives harvesting them. While it may sound revolting to other cultures, it is considered the elixir of good health to the Chinese. They believe it promotes longevity, boosts the libido, enhances the immune system and balances the 'Qi' or energy of the body. Like the shark's fin, it has no flavour of its own. There is reputedly no scientific proof of its medicinal value but the age-old belief in its value as a healing agent and status symbol is steadfast in the Chinese culture. It is usually prepared in a soup with chicken stock or eaten as a dessert. A bowl of high-quality bird's-nest soup in Chinese restaurants can cost up to US$100.

The moon cake commemorates a historical event. It was said that in the 14th century, during the Mongol rule of China in the **Yuan Dynasty** (1280–1368), a Chinese resistance leader hatched a clever plot to overthrow the Mongols. As large gatherings of the Chinese were forbidden by the Mongols, the leader decided to hide secret plans of an uprising against the Mongols inside the moon cakes and distribute them to his compatriots as gifts during the Mid-Autumn Festival. The unsuspecting Mongols were defeated by the rebels and China regained control under the **Ming Dynasty** (1368–1644). Today, as part of the Mid-Autumn Festival, moon cakes are distributed as gifts among friends and families.

Dragon Boat Festival

Probably one of the most visual and exciting festivals, the Dragon Boat Race falls on the fifth day of the fifth lunar month, usually May or June. It is to commemorate the death of **Qu Yuan**, a Chinese poet and statesman of the 4th century BC, who committed suicide in the River Mi Lo as a protest against political corruption. It was said that fishermen raced in their boats to save him by beating drums and throwing rice dumplings in the river to prevent the fish from eating his body. Since then, on the anniversary of his death, this gesture has been re-enacted in a dragon boat race as teams paddle in boats over 10m (33ft) long and ornately carved with dragon heads and tails. Competitive spirit is fierce, with a drummer in each boat coxing the paddlers on as the crowd cheer. The main race is at **Stanley**, with international as well as local participants. Rice dumplings wrapped in bamboo leaves are eaten in Qu Yuan's honour on that day.

Food and Drink

Dubbed as the 'Culinary Capital of Asia', Hong Kong's gastronomic scene is a foodie's paradise, tantalizingly diverse and innovative. From sophisticated fine-dining in Eastern, Western, fusion and international cuisines to street-food outlets serving local delicacies, there is something for everyone and every budget, and food is available at every corner and at all hours. Because of Hong Kong's close proximity to China, Chinese food lovers can sample food from every region in China, with Cantonese as the dominant cuisine. Hong Kong is blessed with an army of incredible Chinese chefs who pride themselves in their innovative and artistic culinary skills, serving up signature dishes from around China.

In fact, all the flavours of the world are showcased here. Japanese food is the most popular Asian food after Chinese, and a plethora of Japanese restaurants with famous international brand names such as Nobu and Zuma have opened their doors here to the well-heeled crowd. In contrast, there are inexpensive Japanese cafés and small outlets serving an array of street food Japanese style.

Below: *A typical array of dim sum dishes served for yum cha, a favourite meal for breakfast and lunch especially among families on weekends.*

Eating Hong Kong Style

For a real dining experience in Hong Kong, eating out in street cafés and stalls is a must. At these informal outlets, known locally as **cha chaan teng** and **dai pai dong**, service is fast and food is wholesome, tasty and served in large portions (enough for two people to share). They operate from early in the morning for breakfast to late at night, with some opening 24 hours. As most of these eateries are fairly small, it might be necessary to share tables during the peak period at lunch time.

It is often said that the Chinese eat anything with legs and wings except tables, chairs and aeroplanes. The street food illustrates that there is a recipe for every part of a farm animal on the menu and the most popular dish is **offal**

DIM SUM – 'TOUCH THE HEART'

Hong Kong is famous for its dim sum (meaning 'touch the heart') dishes – a massive array of small dishes, with deep-fried, baked or steamed meat and seafood usually served in bamboo containers for breakfast and lunch. Signature dim sum dishes not to be missed are *char siu bau*, steamed bun with barbecue pork fillings; *siu mai*, steamed meat dumpling; *har gau*, steamed prawn dumpling; *char siu soh*, baked pastry with barbecue pork fillings; and baked egg tarts for dessert. On Sundays, dim sum restaurants are packed with families having their weekend gathering of *yum cha* (which literally means 'drinking tea' in Chinese) as they feast on the wide variety of dim sum dishes washed down by Chinese tea.

soup, a concoction of lungs, tripe and intestines served with noodles and vegetables – quite an acquired taste for the uninitiated. For the less adventurous, **staple café fares** such as chicken rice (steamed chicken served with rice cooked in chicken stock), fish ball noodle soup, congee rice gruel, baked rice with sweet sour pork, noodle dishes, roast duck and goose are recommended among a vast choice of other local dishes. Hong Kong is famous for its **roast goose**.

All cafés serve Chinese tea when you sit down at a table but the favourite beverages are 'Hong Kong milk', which is strong tea with evaporated milk; *yun-yong*, a concoction of milky tea and coffee; *ning kar*, coffee with lemon; and coconut milk with boiled red beans served cold with ice.

Recreation, Sports, Arts and Entertainment

The people of Hong Kong are renowned for their hardworking and entrepreneurial lifestyle, with activities on the go day and night. But it is not all work and no play. The government is keen to enhance an environment where there are plenty of facilities for recreation, arts, sports and entertainment to improve the population's quality of life. It is quite common to see people early in the morning, particularly the older generation, practising t'ai chi and dance exercises in the parks to keep fit. There are many well-maintained and beautifully landscaped parks around the country for exercise and recreation. The government Home Affairs Bureau has set up various organizations to oversee these functions. The **Sports Commission** advises on all matters related to sport development, while the **Leisure and Cultural Services Department** (LCSD) helps 'to provide leisure and cultural services to the community, preserves its cultural heritage, beautifies its physical environment, and fosters synergy with sports, cultural and community organizations'. It also plays a role in developing Hong Kong as an Asian centre for developing the performing arts, developing creativity and instilling among the people a long-term interest in the arts.

The vibrant performing arts scene exemplifies Hong Kong's position as one of Asia's cultural centres, drawing on the skill of both local and international performers. Culture lovers will be spoilt for choice when it comes to concerts, shows and cultural performances (www.hk.artsfestival.org). The **Hong Kong Cultural Centre** is one of the main venues for performing arts. The **City Contemporary Dance Company** (www.ccdc.com.hk), established in 1979, is a professional modern dance company that brings out the best talent to create dance in the context of modern China. The **Hong Kong Ballet** (www.hkballet.com) stages ballet performances throughout the year, including productions from overseas. The **Hong Kong Chinese Orchestra** (www.hkco.org), founded in 1977, is the only professional, full-scale Chinese orchestra in Hong Kong. Although its main core production is in Chinese music, it has also incorporated a fusion of the musical art of East and West. Its role as cultural ambassador for Hong Kong is strengthened by its overseas tours including visits to Australia, New Zealand and London. The **Hong Kong Philharmonic Orchestra** (www.hkpo.com) with its 90 full-time musicians is one of the finest orchestras in Asia and their concerts, notably Symphony Under the Stars, are much acclaimed and command huge audiences. For a taste of Chinese performing arts, the **Hong Kong Repertory Theatre** (www.hkrep.com) stages productions in Cantonese and Putonghua (Mandarin), with traditional Chinese storylines. Formed in 1977, it is the largest professional theatre company of its kind in Hong Kong.

Below: *An ornately made-up Chinese opera actress performing a scene from a classic tale, often lavishly staged in many Chinese festivals and theatres.*

2
Northern Hong Kong Island

The Central and Western districts of Hong Kong Island reflect the essence of Hong Kong both historically and commercially. There's an air of affluence amid the pulsating rhythm of brisk trading by chic commercial powerhouses encased in glittering skyscrapers of steel and glass. The sophisticated cityscape by the harbour front is one of the most iconic sights in the world. By day it is the nerve centre of the financial and commercial world and by night it is transformed into a wonderland ablaze with thousands of colourful lights. This is the birthplace of Hong Kong as an important trading centre from its humble beginnings as an island with just barren rocks and nothing else. Today, amid its bustling atmosphere and ultramodern skyline, pockets of old Hong Kong still remain under the shadow of the skyscrapers. The hilly narrow streets in the districts reveal a treasure trove of British legacy and old Chinese heritage, and in some quarters the traditional way of life still lingers on.

CENTRAL AND WESTERN DISTRICTS

Exploring the Central and Western districts on foot is a fascinating way to learn about the living culture of Hong Kong Island. It is advisable to wear very comfortable shoes, a hat and light cotton or silk attire when embarking on this walk with its undulating and steep terrain in some parts. The weather is hot and humid especially during the summer months, so take time to rest in the many tea houses and savour the atmosphere. Armed with a city map – available from most hotels

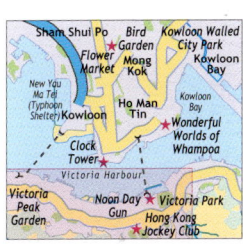

DON'T MISS

*** **The Peak:** the Peak Tram ride and the Sky Terrace.
*** **Central and Western Districts:** colonial legacy.
** **Man Mo Temple:** historical Chinese temple.
*** **The Harbour Front:** wonderful architecture.
*** **The Star Ferry:** take a harbour cruise.
*** **Causeway Bay:** shopping headquarters of Hong Kong.
*** **Tram cars:** see the north coast of Hong Kong Island.
** **Hong Kong Convention and Exhibition Centre** and **Golden Bauhinia Square:** flag raising ceremony.

Opposite: *'Two ifc' building in the financial district.*

Opposite: *Man Mo Temple in Hollywood Road is dedicated to the Taoist God of Literature, Wen Chang, and the God of War, Guan Yu.*

and Hong Kong Tourism Board (HKTB) offices – take a stroll through time and back to the present as you venture through the many faces of these districts.

In the **Western** part of the district, take time to explore the side streets – such as Wing Lok Street, Des Voeux Road West, Ko Shing Street and Bonham Strand West – and browse through shops selling ginseng and birds' nests (*see* panel, page 18), believed to boost energy and prolong longevity. Dried seafood, like the scallops, abalone and oysters so essential to Chinese *haute cuisine*, is stocked in abundance in stores along these roads. There are also many traditional Chinese medicine centres selling herbs, roots and cures for all ailments. It's a visual and olfactory feast of traditional delicacies, all beautifully displayed in glass jars with red tops. Western Market, a distinctive Edwardian-style building at Sheung Wan, is a great place to look for arts, crafts and collectables, while Sheung Wan Fong piazza next to it is surrounded by traditional shops reminiscent of old Hong Kong.

If you're looking for antiques, head to Hollywood Road (a.k.a Antiques Street) and Upper Lascar Row (a.k.a. Cat Street) to hunt for bargains and hidden treasures among the many antique and curios shops. The shops will be happy to arrange for shipment of large items to your home country. Hollywood Road was built in 1844 by the British army and was named after the abundant holly shrubs growing in the area at the time. Nearby is Possession Street (Shui Hang Hau in Chinese), where the British first landed in Hong Kong in 1841.

Man Mo Temple **

Along Hollywood Road at the intersection with Ladder Street is Hong Kong's oldest temple built in the Chinese traditional style during the colonial era (ca. 1848). This small temple is dedicated to the Taoist God of Literature, **Wen Chang** (seen here with his calligraphy brush), and the God of War, **Guan Yu** (holding a sword). The temple also houses the statues of **Pau Kung** (the God of Justice) and **Shing Wong** (the God of the City). The interior is festooned with large conical coils of incense suspended

from the ceiling, filling the temple with thick smoke that swirls around the altars and statues of the various deities, creating a mystical ambience. Devotees light candles and joss sticks, offer prayers and give votive offerings of fruits and cakes to the gods. Historical relics – a bronze bell made during the reign of Emperor Daoguang (1820–50) and imperial sedan chairs made in 1862 – are displayed by the entrance. The sedan chairs were once used to parade the gods through the streets during Chinese festivals. As in most temples in Hong Kong, this is a popular place for **Kau Cim fortune-telling** – shaking a bamboo cylinder until a fortune stick falls out of it. The stick bears inscriptions of your fortune, with the English translation available in a booklet on sale in the temple.

SoHo **

For a lively atmosphere with an abundance of chic restaurants, upbeat bars and cafés, make a beeline for South of Hollywood Road, or SoHo for short. The area consists of Shelley Street, Elgin Street, Peel Street, Staunton Street and Old Bailey Street.

The 800m-long (2625ft) **Central-Mid-Levels Escalator**, declared the world's longest covered escalator by the *Guinness Book of Records*, is an experience. A journey along its entire length takes about 20 minutes and it operates one-way downhill from 06:00 to 10:00 and then uphill from 10:20 until midnight. It serves as a transit link for residences of the Mid-Levels, an area midway between the Peak and the waterfront. It is advisable to travel on it after 09:00 when the morning rush hour is over.

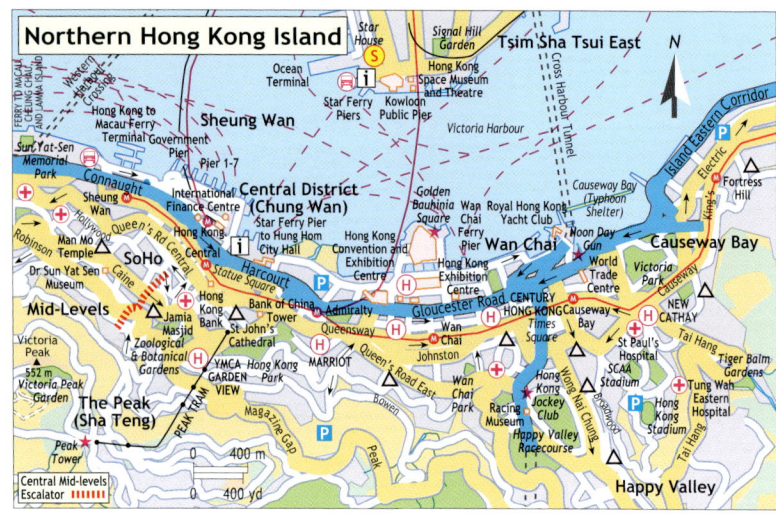

Dr Sun Yat Sen Museum **

While at Mid-Levels, follow the sign to the Dr Sun Yat Sen Museum at 7 Castle Road. Dedicated to Dr Sun Yat Sen, the famous revolutionary and Father of Modern China, this museum is located in the historic **Kom Tong Hall**, a handsome building completed in 1914 in a blend of Chinese and Western architectural styles. A very grand building with beautiful interior wooden structures, sweeping staircase and stained-glass windows, it houses over a hundred invaluable historical artefacts and photographs, complemented with multimedia programmes, charting the life of this renowned statesman and the modernization and revolutionary path of Hong Kong in the late 1900s. The 'Dr Sun Yat Sen and Modern China' permanent exhibition features the extraordinary life of Dr Sun, from an aspiring medical student to a legendary revolutionary who brought social and political changes to modern China. It highlights his close relationship with Hong Kong where he was educated and where he set up his base to plan his revolution, which eventually overthrew the Qing Dynasty and formed the Republic of China. The museum is open Mon–Wed and Fri–Sat

LAN KWAI FONG

While SoHo has its appeal by day and night, Lan Kwai Fong by D'Aguilar Street in Central is the place to be when the lights are low and you are in a party mood. The place is buzzing with clubs, funky bars, pubs and restaurants that swell up with crowds of merrymakers and drinkers partying till the crack of dawn. It is party central for the 'in-crowds' and night owls.

10:00–18:00, Sun and public holidays 10:00–19:00; closed on Thu (except public holidays) and the first two days of Chinese New Year. Concession tickets are available for full-time students, the disabled and senior citizens aged 60 or above; children under four are free (e-mail: sysm@lcsd.gov.hk website: http://hk.drsunyat sen.museum).

St John's Cathedral *

The wide steps of Duddell Street, with its last remaining four gas lamps installed between 1875 and 1889, lead to Battery Path where St John's Cathedral is located at the intersection with Garden Road. Built in the shape of a cross in a 13th-century early English and decorated Gothic architectural style, it was completed in 1849. Dedicated to St John the Evangelist, it is the oldest surviving Western religious building in Hong Kong and is reputed to be the oldest Anglican church in the Far East. A tower was added to the front of the church in 1873. The church has three beautiful stained-glass windows with the crucifixion of Christ depicted in the east window facing the main entrance. It was declared a national monument in 1996. On Christmas Day in 1941 in the midst of the Japanese attack on Hong Kong, the Reverend Alaric Rose was conducting a service at the cathedral. It is said he continued with the service while the shelling was in full flow outside. It was also here that the first service was conducted after the liberation of Hong Kong from the Japanese by the British Royal Navy on 19 September 1945. During the occupation, the Japanese took over the cathedral for their own community use. Services in the cathedral today are conducted in English and Mandarin.

THE PEAK

Just down Garden Road from St John's Cathedral is the Lower Peak Tram Terminus to Victoria Peak. A visit to the Peak is a must. It is the highest point on the island and was used as a signal post for incoming ships in the 19th century. It was and still is the exclusive residential

---

THREE MICHELIN STARS FOR A 'VIEW OF THE DRAGON'

Michelin Guide's first edition of their Hong Kong Macau 2009 guide has granted a three-star accolade to the Four Seasons Hotel's Chinese restaurant, **Lung King Heen**. This is the first time Michelin has included a Chinese restaurant in its guide and Lung King Heen is the only restaurant in Hong Kong to have been given this prestigious award of a three-star rating. Its executive chef, **Chan Yan Tak**, became the first Chinese chef in the world to receive the coveted Michelin three-star award. Lung King Heen, or 'View of the Dragon', epitomizes the intricacy and sophistication of Cantonese cuisine at its best, with the emphasis on dim sum, seafood and seasonal delicacies based on traditional and imperial recipes created with a contemporary touch. The restaurant is elegantly designed in glass and silver decor inspired by the dazzle of the Hong Kong skyline, accented with Chinese antiques and a central showpiece of a 2m-high (7ft) silk and glass screen depicting a traditional Chinese landscape inspired by a Suen Dynasty painting.

enclave for the wealthy, where the weather is cooler and the scenery is stunning. It was exclusively reserved for expatriates from 1904–47. Before the tram was built, the wealthy residents used to travel up and down the peak in sedan chairs carried by their staff and coolies. In 1881, Alexander Finlay Smith, who had worked for the Scottish Highland Railways, petitioned the then Governor, Sir John Pope-Hennessy, to operate the tram route. It was officially opened by Governor Sir George William des Voeux on 30 May 1888.

The Peak Tower and Sky Terrace ***

The Peak Tram terminates at the Peak Tower, which stands at 428m (1404ft) above sea level, with the entire rooftop dedicated to the Sky Terrace, the crowning glory of the Peak. The wok-shaped structure is one of the most avant-garde and stylish buildings in Hong Kong, with a touch of the futuristic sci-fi look. It was originally built in 1971 but it went through many changes throughout the years. In 2005, the Peak Tower was upgraded and transformed into a leisure destination with shops, restaurants, speciality and interactive entertainment, including game arcades. The main attraction here is **Madame Tussauds**, which features waxworks of international and local stars, notably David Beckham, Jackie Chan and the late Bruce Lee, Hong Kong's most famous kung fu master and actor.

A visit to the Peak Tower is not complete without experiencing the view from the **Sky Terrace** with its stunning 360-degree vista of Hong Kong Island, Tsim Sha Tsui area in Kowloon and beyond. It tends to be quite misty and hazy in the daytime but the nightscape from this vantage point is not to be missed. For photographers, this is the best site for taking pictures of Victoria Harbour and the city skyline, especially night shots. There is also a **Sky Gallery** showcasing works of the city's talented artists. Admission to the Sky Terrace requires a separate ticket, which can be purchased at the Lower Peak Tram Terminus as part of your tram fare or at the Peak Tower (see At A Glance, page 48).

Left: *Peak Tower, with its futuristic-looking structure, is a must for visitors to observe the magnificent view of the harbour and Kowloon, especially at night.*

Statue Square and Financial District ★★★

Down the hill from the Peak Terminus lies the financial nerve centre and the seat of power of the government, the Legislative Council (Legco) and Statue Square. Built at the end of the 19th century, Statue Square is surrounded by iconic buildings, notably the **Hong Kong and Shanghai Bank** (HSBC), the **Bank of China** and the **Legco** building. The name of the square was derived from the installation of the statues of **Queen Victoria** and other royals but, during the Japanese occupation, they were looted and dispatched to Japan to be melted down. After the war, most of the statues remained intact and were returned. The statue of Queen Victoria is now sited in Victoria Park in Causeway Bay. Today, the statue of **Sir Thomas Jackson**, manager-in-chief of HSBC Bank from 1876–1902, stands in the middle of the square overlooked by the Legco building. Victoria Harbour used to be visible from here but with reclamations and new buildings in the way, the harbour view is now obstructed. At the northern end of the square lies the **Cenotaph** in honour of the dead of World War II. The square is a popular place for the locals to seek respite from the bustling city and the favourite Sunday gathering point for the many Filipino domestic workers to socialize.

Soaring 180m (591ft) high, the **HSBC building** casts a shadow over the square. One of the oldest skyscrapers of Hong Kong and built by **Sir Norman Foster**, it is 47

THE PEAK TRAM

A journey on the Peak Tram is one of the highlights of Hong Kong. This iconic mode of transport operates on a double reversible funicular system with the automatically managed tram car speed travelling at 6m (20ft) per second. The Lower Terminus is 28m (92ft) and the Upper Terminus 396m (1300ft) above sea level. The length of the track is 1365m (4480ft) with a track gradient from 4 to 27 degrees. Today, it transports more than 7 million passengers per annum with an average of 11,000 people per day. The 15-minute ride climbs up steep terrain, past narrow streets with condominiums and forested areas with a glimpse of the sea along the way. Sit on the right-hand side of the tram to get a sea view on your way up the peak and vice versa on the way down.

Above: *Symphony of Lights is a nightly performance – a visual feast of laser lights spot-lighted on famous buildings on the harbour front, accompanied by music and narration.*

storeys high and was built between 1978 and 1985. Underneath the building, guarded by two stone lions, is a public space the size of a cathedral, another favourite meeting point for Filipinos on Sundays.

Sprouting up adjacent to HSBC is the **Bank Of China**, one of the most unique and architecturally intriguing buildings in Hong Kong. Designed by world-renowned architect **I M Pei**, it was started in 1985 and completed in 1990. This shining tower of glass and aluminium, made up of geometrical and triangular panels which change shape as it soars to a dizzy height of 369m (1211ft), is topped by two antennae, dubbed by some locals as the 'devil's horns'. The sharp angles and glass panels catch the sun during the day and are emblazoned with lights at night like a beacon on Victoria Harbour. Its 70 storeys are built around an atrium, and visitors can go to the **Sky Deck** on the 42nd floor to catch a bird's-eye view of Hong Kong. The unusual building is supposed to represent a bamboo plant with its segmented stems, as bamboo is an auspicious plant in Chinese culture symbolizing growth and longevity.

Though dwarfed by all the skyscrapers around it, the **Legislative Council Building** stands out with its neo-classical architecture. Designed by **Sir Aston Webb**, it was completed in 1912 and used as the Supreme Court until 1985 when it was taken over by the Legislative Council. This beautiful building, with its imposing dome and rows of columns, is topped by a statue of 'Justice' symbolized by the Greek goddess Themis presiding over the main entrance. It was declared a historical monument and looks stunning when lit up at night.

THE HARBOUR FRONT ***

A stroll along the harbour front is the best way to take in the architectural marvel of the city skyline, though you might end up with a neck ache from prolonged staring up at the many wonderful buildings. The most imposing is the International Finance Centre at Finance Street known as **'Two ifc' building**. It dominates the skyline at 420m (1378ft) high with an 88-storey obelisk shape, ranking among the highest buildings in the world. The imposing tower, designed by **Cesar Pelli**, culminates in a sculptural crown said to symbolize a 'Welcome to the City' and a shimmering beacon at Victoria Harbour. It has 22 trading floors and commands a panoramic vista of Victoria Harbour, Kowloon and beyond. Its sister building, **'One ifc'**, is smaller and less impressive, standing at only 210m (689ft) high with 39 storeys including four trading floors. Nearby is the ifc shopping mall with over 200 international brands and a cinema. It is considered the 'No. 1 living and entertainment mega-structure in the city', with retail therapy on overdrive.

WAN CHAI DISTRICT
Wan Chai ***

Much of present-day Wan Chai is reclaimed land stretching from Queen's Road East to the Convention and Exhibition Centre area over a distance of 1km (0.6 mile), spanning a 100-year time frame. The original reclamation started in 1842–90 for residential development and continued in the 1960s. By the 1990s, it extended over six separate reclamation projects including the landmark building of the **Hong Kong Convention and Exhibition Centre**. It has evolved from a humble fishing village to a thriving business district today, albeit not on the same grand scale as in Central, and is a good place to get a glimpse of the nostalgic old Hong Kong lifestyle with the many streets and alleyways of markets, restaurants and shops selling traditional Chinese wares. **Tai Yuen Street Market** is a lively place, with stalls selling local dried food and household products at bargain prices.

THE STAR FERRY

Dorabjee Naorojee Mithaiwala, a Parsee businessman, started the ferry service in 1880 with just one steam-fuelled ferry plying between Victoria Harbour and Kowloon, the crossing taking up to an hour. He called it the *Morning Star* under his company, the **Kowloon Ferry Company**. By 1890, the fleet had increased to four single-deck ferries, later upgraded to double-deckers. It was taken over by **Star Ferry Company** in 1898, named after the ferries that have 'Star' in their names. The company today boasts 12 ferries plying between Tsim Sha Tsui and Central; Tsim Sha Tsui and Wan Chai; Hung Hom and Central; and Hung Hom and Wan Chai. The famous green-and-white double-decker ferries are the cheapest way to cross the harbour and the most enjoyable way to view the harbour skyline, albeit the journey takes only a few minutes. Star Ferry also offers an hour-long harbour cruise (tel: 852 2118 6208, e-mail: harbour tour@starferry.com.hk).

Wan Chai gained notoriety in the novel *The World of Suzie Wong* by Richard Mason in 1957, which portrays the seedy world of girlie bars and brothels serving the British and American soldiers on R&R during that period. Today it is still famous for its nightlife in Lockhart Road but the seedy bars and brothels have been replaced mostly by funky clubs and bars.

Blue House *

Built in the 1870s, it was originally the Wah Tor Community Medical Centre providing traditional Chinese medicine to local people, believed to be the first hospital of its kind at the time. When the hospital closed down in 1886, it was used as a temple dedicated to the namesake of the hospital, **Wah Tor**, a revered ancient Chinese doctor. It was demolished in the 1910s and rebuilt as a four-storey tenement block in the 1920s. In the 1950s it was used as a martial arts school by followers of the legendary martial art master and revolutionary **Wong Fei Hung**. In the 1970s the government took over the renovation and painted the house blue, which gave rise to its present name. Sitting tenants still live in the building, but it is earmarked to be developed into a museum along with other historic buildings in the Stone Nullah Lane area.

Below: *The ultramodern Hong Kong Convention and Exhibition Centre, designed with a roof like a seabird in flight, is one of the most famous buildings on the harbour front.*

Hong Kong Convention and Exhibition Centre (HKCEC) **

Probably the most famous landmark on the waterfront at Victoria Harbour, the HKCEC was opened in November 1988 and, due to its great success as Asia's best convention and exhibition centre, it was expanded in 1997. A 40,000m² (430,556-sq-ft) aluminium-clad roof was added, sculpted to portray a sea bird soaring in flight. It is one of the most architecturally fascinating buildings in Hong Kong. It has a total area of 221,969m² (2,389,254 sq ft) with over 70,000m² (753,473 sq ft) of rentable space for functions. A second expansion, which began in 2006, has added an additional 19,400m² (208,820 sq ft) for conventions, exhibitions, meetings, large banquets and entertainment. The state-of-the-art centre has two swimming pools, a garden, running track, tennis court, golf driving range and health club to service the adjacent hotels and service apartments. There are three restaurants: the **Congress Restaurant** serving international cuisine, the **Golden Bauhinia** with Chinese cuisine and the **Harbour Kitchen** serving local favourites. The Grand Foyer at the entrance of the Grand Hall is a great venue from which to admire the stunning harbour views.

Golden Bauhinia Square **

History was made on this square at midnight on 30 June 1997 when Britain officially handed Hong Kong over to China after 150 years of colonial rule, officially known as the '**Hong Kong Handover**'. Just before midnight, the British Union Flag and the Hong Kong colonial flag were lowered to the strain of the British national anthem, *God Save the Queen*, and at the stroke of midnight the flags of the People's Republic of China and the new regional flag of Hong Kong were raised to the rousing tune of *March Of The Volunteers*, the country's national anthem. Amid much celebration, Hong Kong officially returned to the motherland on the morning of 1 July 1997, the birth of the **Hong Kong Special Administrative Region**. To mark this momentous occasion in history, the Chinese government presented the 'Forever Blooming'

BAUHINIA (*BAUHINIA BLAKEANA*)

Also known as the 'Hong Kong orchid tree', this species of bauhinia is endemic to Hong Kong and is named after **Sir Henry Blake**, the British governor of Hong Kong from 1898 to 1903. He was a keen botanist. The plant was reputedly discovered at **Telegraph Bay** on Hong Kong Island in the 19th century, and its orchid-like purple flower is the emblem of Hong Kong. The tree has two-lobe oval-shaped leaves resembling a butterfly, considered by the Chinese as a symbol of intelligence. It is said that students using its leaves as bookmarks will be inspired in their studies. Bauhinias are found in abundance in parks, along roadsides and around the countryside. The flower is also the motif on the Hong Kong flag, with the petals pointing in a clockwise direction. Each petal has a red star, the symbol of communism and socialism. The flower is portrayed in white against a background of red to identify with the flag of the PRC; red is also regarded as an auspicious colour in Chinese culture. The two colours denote one country with two systems.

FLAG RAISING CEREMONY

Witnessed by hundreds of tourists every day, the flag raising ceremony in Golden Bauhinia Square starts at 07:50 and finishes by 08:03. Five police officers dressed in their standard uniforms perform the raising of the flags to the national anthem. According to protocol, the flag of the PRC is raised first, followed by the Hong Kong flag. The PRC flag always flies higher than the Hong Kong flag and in a more prominent position. On the second Sunday of every month, this ceremony is conducted by various youth groups. On the first day of the month from 07:45–08:13 a more elaborate ceremony is carried out by 15 police officers accompanied by a 10-man rifle unit in ceremonial uniforms. The national anthem is played by the Police Band followed by a 10-minute performance by the Police Pipe Band. The flag is lowered at 18:00 with the same pomp and ceremony, with the Hong Kong flag being lowered first. The ceremony is not carried out in bad weather. To get to the square, go to Wan Chai MTR Exit A5 and look for the sign.

Golden Bauhinia sculpture to Hong Kong. In the likeness of the emblematic flower of Hong Kong, the bauhinia, clad in gold, it stands proudly outside HKCEC on Expo Promenade. The daily raising and lowering of the country's flags are conducted here (see panel, this page), a popular tourist attraction. This is also the best vantage point from which to observe the Symphony of Lights (see panel, page 28) on the Kowloon side. Near the Golden Bauhinia Square is the Reunification Monument bearing the inscription of President Jiang Zemin's calligraphy.

CAUSEWAY BAY ★★★

This area is notable for its fashionable shops, malls with many flagship stores and great eating places. The real estate in the shopping area is considered to be among the most expensive in the world. One of Hong Kong's swankiest shopping malls, **Times Square**, is the main attraction here. Opened in April 1994, it's an ultramodern building equipped with state-of-the-art technology and crowned by imposing twin towers rising at 46 and 39 storeys high. The impressive frontage has columns and a giant clock. It is billed as a 'one-stop shopping and entertainment centre', spread over 16 floors with 230 upscale shops, a multicomplex cinema and recreational and dining areas. The rest of the buildings are prime office spaces. This is party central for the New Year's Eve countdown.

Noon Day Gun ★

Nearby, at the harbour, is the **Causeway Bay Typhoon Shelter**, a pretty cove where luxury yachts berth alongside Chinese junks and pleasure boats for tourists. Access to this area is via the underground car park at Excelsior Hotel. The Noon Day Gun is sited here, the remnant of a colonial legacy. The original site at East Point, now reclaimed, had been there since the 1860s when Jardines used to fire the gun salute to welcome the head of the company or important merchants when they sailed into port. It was said that the Royal Navy protested against this practice as they felt that it was the preserve of senior officers of the armed services or

Opposite: *Times Square mall, a massive complex, is the main shopping and entertainment hub in Causeway Bay.*

government officials. As a penalty, Jardines was ordered to fire the gun as a time signal at noon. The tradition is still being carried out today in its present site. The original gun was dismantled by the Japanese when they occupied the island in 1941 but after the war, the Royal Navy presented Jardines with another cannon, which had seen action in World War I, and the service was back in operation on 1 July 1947. The Noon Day Gun was immortalized in Noel Coward's song, *Mad Dogs and Englishmen*, and it is said that he had the honour of firing the gun in 1968 on one of his visits to Hong Kong.

Victoria Park **

Along the promenade from the Typhoon Shelter area is Victoria Park, the largest park on Hong Kong Island. The park was opened in 1957 and named after Queen Victoria whose seated statue today presides over the park by the seafront. During the Japanese occupation the statue, along with other statues from Statue Square, was spirited off to Japan to be melted down, but it remained intact and was returned after the war. Spanning an area of 19ha (47 acres), the park is landscaped with over 5500 trees and flowering plants. It is often used by demonstrators and soapbox speakers airing their views to an audience. While the Filipino domestic workers swarm on Statue Square every Sunday for their gatherings, the Indonesian workers congregate at Victoria Park for their Sunday social meeting and create quite a curious sight with their weekly giant picnic in the park. The park has a bandstand, a pebble walking trail, sports facilities and fast-food kiosks. It is a great place to relax and enjoy the sea view and the breeze.

HAPPY VALLEY RACECOURSE

Built over reclaimed marshland in 1846, the racecourse was improved in 1931 and modernized and redesigned in 1995 with a new grass racetrack, a new grandstand, a Jockey Club and the Hong Kong Racing Museum. In 2001 LED monitors were installed, upgrading it to a world-class racecourse. Horse racing is the most popular spectator sport in Hong Kong and the buzz among the avid gamblers on race day is infectious. Adjoining the stands is the **Hong Kong Racing Museum** charting the history and development of horse racing at Happy Valley and Sha Tin, the other racecourse on Kowloon side (*see page 75*). The museum opens from 10:00–17:00 (closed Mon and Chinese New Year holidays). Nearest MTR is Causeway Bay with a 20-minute walk along Wong Nai Chung Road.

3
Southern Hong Kong Island

The south coast of Hong Kong Island is defined by forested hills punctuated by picturesque bays and coves. Exposed to the openness of the South China Sea without the advantage of a hinterland protection like in Kowloon or deep-water harbour as enjoyed by Victoria Harbour on the northern coast, it is less commercial and more residential. Sandy bays along the shoreline and steep hillsides with stunning sea views make this region a desirable and expensive residential enclave, particularly around Repulse Bay. Prime locations such as Ocean Park, Aberdeen, Repulse Bay and Stanley are popular leisure destinations for the locals and visitors. Although the MTR does not stretch that far, there are regular and efficient bus services from Central to service these areas. The bus ride is a great way to enjoy the view along the way. The south coast offers a respite from the bustle of the city and the north coast and affords an enjoyable day out.

OCEAN PARK ***

Spanning an area of 870,000m² (215 acres) at the tip of a headland with undulating terrain, Ocean Park offers a stunning view of the sea and islets in this region. It was opened in January 1977 by the then Governor of Hong Kong, Sir Murray MacLehose, funded by the Hong Kong Jockey Club on land courtesy of the Hong Kong Government. It is run by a statutory body and non-profit organization, the **Ocean Park Corporation**, and it offers a balanced mix of 'entertainment, education and conservation facilities to guests'.

DON'T MISS

*** Ocean Park: a marine theme park with a conservation mission; birds and pandas are among the attractions.
*** Stanley: an escape from the shadows of the city skyscrapers to a village atmosphere with a great market.
** Aberdeen: enjoy a culinary experience at Jumbo Kingdom and also a harbour cruise.
** Repulse Bay: a relaxing day out to one of Hong Kong's best beaches away from the city.

Opposite: *Aberdeen Harbour is home to the Tanka boat people.*

OCEAN PARK FUTURE DEVELOPMENT

A Master Redevelopment Project was unveiled in March 2005 to further expand and improve the park by doubling the number of attractions, enabling Ocean Park to establish itself as a world-class must-see landmark of Hong Kong. The HK$5.5 billion project was put into action in November 2006 and is scheduled to be completed in six years over eight phases while the park remains in operation. Future projects include the building of three hotels – Ocean Hotel near the Entry Plaza, Fisherman's Wharf at Tai Shue Wan and Spa Hotel at the summit area. A funicular system called the Ocean Express is now being built in a 1.2km (0.75-mile) tunnel across Brick Hill, parallel to the cable car. When completed, it will transport visitors from the waterfront to the summit in just three minutes. The journey will include multimedia and interactive entertainment about marine life and wildlife conservation to project the park's principles to 'promote conservation and bring guests closer to nature'.

As part of its aim, Ocean Park is fully committed to scientific research of its unique collection of insects, fish, birds and marine mammals. It has a record of successful breeding programmes of rare shark species, bottlenose dolphins, sea lions, sea horses and different species of sea jellies. Endangered birds and butterflies are also being hatched and reared at the park. Under the **Ocean Park Conservation Foundation Hong Kong**, it advocates, facilitates and participates in the conservation of wildlife and habitats, with an emphasis on Asia, through research and education. It runs educational tours for school children and teachers under the **Ocean Park Academy** and also offers a 'Clean Air Programme' through a mobile **Clean Air Outreach** exhibition to over 80 schools and 9000 students annually.

A precursor to Hong Kong Disneyland®, it is a marine and animal theme park with attractions divided into three geographical categories: the **Lowland**, the **Headland** and **Tai Shue Wan**, which are connected by cable car and an outdoor escalator, second longest after Central-Mid-Levels.

The Lowland

Dedicated to children, this area features **Kid's World**, 14,200m² (3.5 acres) of amusement park with Whiskers Theatre showcasing sea lions, a merry-go-round, Interactive Shadow Play area, remote-control cars and boats and Tiny Town Games involving skilled games. At the corner of the park is the **Dolphin University** where guests can observe and learn about dolphin behaviour at close quarters. It is fun for families with young children.

The highlight of the Lowland is the **Hong Kong Jockey Club Giant Panda Habitat**. The pandas – named An An, Jia Jia, Ying Ying and Le Le – were gifts from the Central People's Government of China to the people of Hong Kong. The newly furbished enclosure is divided into two sections, housing two pandas in each, and is designed to reflect their natural habitat in Sichuan. Visitors can view the pandas through a glass wall, observing them at play and feasting on bamboo leaves. They are a delight to watch and it is easy to understand why these extraordinary-looking creatures are such a huge attraction world-wide and why their dwindling number in the wild is a major concern among wildlife conservationists.

The Headland

The Headland show-cases the main theme of the park, with its marine exhibits and various rides combining education with entertainment and fun. The highlight here is **Sea Dreams Theatre at Ocean Park** with an amusing show consisting of dolphins and seals displaying their skill and intelligence by interacting with their human co-stars. Check out the times of performances at the theatre.

One of the most popular attractions here is the **Atoll Reef** with its unique exhibitions of the marine life of the Indo-Pacific coral island. Housed in a giant aquarium over four levels of viewing galleries, it features 1500 fish of 250 species, including 22 giant Napoleon fish (the largest collection in the world of this species), graceful stingrays gliding through the waters like alien space-crafts, and sharks patrolling the reef among hundreds of colourful reef fish. Stop and observe the wondrous underwater world and let the crowd go by in the gallery.

Ocean Park boasts Southeast Asia's first stand-alone **sea jelly exhibition**, with more than 1000 jellyfish. They are displayed in eight different exhibit zones with state-of-the-art theatrical lighting, multimedia sound-track and visual special effects to capture the magical beauty of these fascinating marine invertebrates. Another newly introduced attraction is the **Chinese Sturgeon Aquarium**. These fish are considered to be the

HALLOWEEN IN OCEAN PARK

Ocean Park is famous for its celebration of Halloween in October. The whole park is elaborately themed with ghoulish displays, haunted houses and scary thrills lurking around every corner. The staff members are dressed as ghostly creatures to amuse, scare and whip the guests into Halloween frenzy. The park stays open till 23:30 to accommodate the revellers who can join in the fun by dressing up for the occasion. It is a highlight for the locals, and on the weekend of Halloween the park is packed with party-goers, all out to have a hauntingly good time.

'national treasures' of China and 'living fossils' (sturgeons have survived since the age of the dinosaurs over 140 million years ago). Visitors can have a close look at these rare species via an 11.5m-long (38ft) travelator round the aquarium.

The **Pacific Pier** is home to the sea lions and seals kept in an environment based on their natural habitat, emulating a northern Californian pier with boardwalks traversing through a rocky shoreline. Visitors can enjoy an edutainment and interactive oceanarium experience observing fish-feeding sessions and learning about the fascinating facts of marine life.

Don't miss the **Ocean Park Tower**, one of the tallest observation towers in Southeast Asia, standing at 200m (565ft) above sea level with 72 floors. The tower affords a stunning 360-degree vista across the South China Sea, notably of Aberdeen, Victoria Harbour and the outlying islands of Lantau, Lamma and Cheung Chau.

The Headland is also the terminal for the **cable car** with 252 cars capable of transporting 4000 visitors per hour from the Lowland. The eight-minute ride reveals a breathtaking view of Deep Water Bay and Repulse Bay along the picturesque headland. It is a great opportunity to capture the stunning landscape on camera from the air.

Below: The cable cars linking the Lowland to the Headland in Ocean Park are an exciting ride, affording a spectacular view of Deep Water Bay and Repulse Bay.

There are various rides and for adrenaline junkies the Dragon – a super-high-speed roller coaster with nasty twists and turns through two giant loops on a 842m-long (921yd) track for maximum thrill – is a must. For an even more heart-thumping moment, try the **Abyss Turbo Drop** where passengers are transported up the tower to a height of 62m (203ft) in just

20 to 25 seconds, then have a brief stop at the top and finally plummet downwards at 65km (40 miles) per hour with a G-force of minus one, said to be even faster than a free fall.

Tai Shue Wan

Situated by the side entrance of Ocean Park, this area is home to the aviaries with about 700 **birds** from over 60 species, many of which are endangered, in this natural habitat of over 17,000m² (4.2 acres). The **Flamingo Pond** features a beautiful collection of 40 pink flamingoes from Africa and Central America. The amusement here is provided by the **Mine Train**, 678m (741yd) of twisting, climbing and dipping track, perched on a cliff overlooking Aberdeen Harbour. The **Raging River** is a thrilling ride, shooting rapids among tropical waterfalls along narrow ravines and ending by shooting down a slide at almost 60km (37 miles) per hour. The **Space Wheel**, at 20m (66ft) high, offers a spectacular ride for thrill-seekers. There are enough exciting rides to satisfy even the die-hard adrenaline junkies.

The 225m-long (246yd) outdoor covered escalator links Tai Shue Wan to the Headland and Middle Kingdom. Ocean Park is open Mon–Sat 10:00–18:00 (except 2 Oct when it opens 10:00–20:00), Sun and public holidays 09:30–18:00. Children under three are free. The admission fee includes most facilities and attractions except skill and coin-operated games.

ABERDEEN **

Next to Ocean Park is Aberdeen, the largest satellite town in Hong Kong, with a population of 60,000. It was named in 1845 after **George Hamilton-Gordon**, the 4th Earl of Aberdeen, the then British Secretary of State for War and the Colonies. Aberdeen is known to the locals as Hong Kong Tsai or Hong Kong Minor and it was here that Hong Kong or Fragrant Harbour got its name – incense trees (*Aquilaria sinensis*) from the New Territories used to be transferred here at the harbour for export to other cities in China. It was a pirates' hideout two centuries ago before a

REPULSE BAY HOTEL (1920–82)

Listed among the grand dames like Raffles in Singapore and the E&O Hotel in Penang, Repulse Bay Hotel in its heyday was the centre of elegant living for the wealthy and famous. The spectacular landscape and impeccable service earned it its place as a favourite haunt for expatriates in Hong Kong and the Far East, and it even attracted international travellers. It is said that the favourite entertainment for the guests here was to do the Charleston, a dance craze in the 1920s. The hotel played host to royals and celebrities, notably Noel Coward and George Bernard Shaw. The late Hollywood actor Marlon Brando was a guest here in the 1950s. Repulse Bay Hotel was immortalized in the Hollywood classic film *Love Is A Many Splendoured Thing* starring William Holden, and also in the Oscar-winning film *Coming Home* with Peter Sellers. The Repulse Bay is now a residential community (*see* page 44).

Above: *The Jumbo Kingdom, a giant floating restaurant, dominates Aberdeen Harbour with its imposing structure styled after an imperial Chinese palace.*

fishing village was established. Today, at its Bei Fung Tong Typhoon Shelter, Aberdeen Harbour is cheek by jowl with luxury yachts, pleasure boats, sampans and the boat people. The harbour is dominated by Jumbo Kingdom, a giant floating complex with dining and conference facilities.

Jumbo Kingdom ***

The Jumbo Kingdom was established in 1976 by Dr Stanley Ho, the renowned entrepreneur famed for his casinos in Macau. It was built with imperial grandeur in the style of an ancient Chinese palace, in a garish rhapsody of red and gold, complete with two celestial golden dragons wrapped round giant pillars at the entrance and topped with a pagoda-style roof. It is one of the most iconic landmarks in Hong Kong and very popular with both tourists and locals. At night, the four-storey floating 'Theme Park On The Sea' is one of the most celebrated sights in Aberdeen Harbour, glittering with thousands of fairy lights, setting the harbour ablaze with its glow. It has been graced by many celebrities (such as John Wayne and Tom Cruise) and royals (including Queen Elizabeth II) and has served as a film location. It has been upgraded and refurbished to include a fine-dining Chinese restaurant, the **Dragon Court**; a cooking academy; conference and banqueting facilities, popular for wedding receptions; and the **Chinese Tea Garden**, for tea ceremonies and tasting. It also offers Sampan Dining where guests can experience a classic Hong Kong traditional style of dining on a sampan with food prepared from the restaurant. On the highest floor, **Top Deck**, a café diner and bar serving international cuisine and seafood, is a fabulous place to enjoy the harbour view at night.

Aberdeen Harbour is home to the boat people known as **Tanka**, an ethnic group from the coastal region of southern China. Traditionally, they have always lived in boats. Through land reclamation, high-rise buildings have sprouted up around the harbour and the younger generation of Tanka people have moved ashore but the older generations still maintain a floating community, living in houseboats as fishermen. If you are touring the harbour on a sampan, it is sometimes possible to take a peek at their houseboats but take care not to invade their privacy.

There are many sampan tours at the pier; check the fare before embarking on one.

There are free boat shuttle services to Jumbo Kingdom from Aberdeen Ferry Pier and Shum Wan Ferry Pier. To get to Aberdeen, take bus 70 from Exchange Square Bus Terminal in Central (Hong Kong MTR Exit D, adjacent to Central MTR) or bus 75 at Exchange Square Bus Terminal to Shum Wan Ferry Pier. From Causeway Bay, take bus 72, 42 or 38 from 500 Hennessy Road to Aberdeen Ferry Pier or bus 72A to Shum Wan Ferry Pier.

REPULSE BAY **

This expansive crescent of golden sand is the most picturesque and one of the most expensive residential areas of Hong Kong, matched only by the Peak. It is said that the British named it Repulse Bay in the 19th century when the Royal Navy used to repulse pirates in the area. The clear warm water is provided with a safety barrier against sharks and floating platforms to accommodate swimmers. It is a very well-kept **beach** with barbecue facilities and lifeguards on duty. At the far end of the beach on the eastern side is an enclave dedicated to various **Chinese deities** and the seascape is dominated by a pair of giant statues of **Tin Hau**, Queen of Heaven and Protector of Seafarers, and **Kwan Yin**, Goddess of Mercy. It is a mini spiritual theme park of the popular Chinese pantheon, including **Fu Lok Sau**, the three Gods of Wisdom, Authority and Longevity; a statue of **Buddha**; and an ornate pavilion protected

STANLEY DRAGON BOAT RACE

This annual event started as a boat race among the local fishermen to celebrate the festival of Tuen Ng, honouring the death anniversary of a great statesman in ancient China. By the late 1960s it began to attract the interest of the expat community in the Stanley area and by the 1970s they had formed their own team to compete with the local Chinese. The event grew so big that the Stanley Dragon Boat Association was formed to manage the race. Today it is a major event in the festival calendar and is open to international participants. The dragon boats are much revered among the Chinese and they have to be blessed with great pomp and ceremony before every race to 'wake up the dragons'. The ritual is officiated by a Taoist monk with chanting of prayers and burning of paper bills known as 'hell money' to appease the gods and to ask for their blessing. Race boats are made of teak with detachable dragon head and tail made of camphor wood and a capacity of 22 crew including a coxswain and a drummer. Only after the blessing can the boats be used in the race. After the race, the boats have to be put to rest for the next year with another ritual of 'resting the dragon' by burning hell money and chanting prayers to thank the gods.
www.dragonboat.org.hk

by six **Foo Dogs**, the celestial guardians of buildings and temples. It is advisable to avoid going to the beach over weekends and public holidays when it will be very crowded with locals who flock here to relax with their families. The beach was developed and improved with artificial sand in 1910. Today it is a pristine stretch of beach very popular with locals and tourists and a great place to watch the sunset.

Across the road from the beach is **The Repulse Bay**, a residential community with two blocks of luxury apartments, just metres from the beach. Its elevated position, backed by a scenic mountain range, commands a stunning view of the sea. This landscape (with the sea in front and the mountain behind) is said to enjoy the most auspicious feng shui configuration. Its most famous apartment block was built with a 'hole in the wall' to allow the 'mountain dragon to fly through the gap to drink at the sea'. It is the most recognized building in Repulse Bay and with its quirky architecture often attracts a lot of attention from visitors.

The Repulse Bay was built on the site of the former **Repulse Bay Hotel** (*see* panel, page 41). The residential community has its own private club with sporting and recreational facilities, swimming pools and restaurants to cater to the luxury lifestyle of the residents. The restaurants – The Verandah, Spices and The Garden – are open to the public. Serviced apartments are available for short- and long-term lease.

Above: *The 'hole in the wall' building in Repulse Bay is a curious feature reputedly built according to feng shui principles and lyrically described as 'allowing the mountain dragon to fly through the gap to drink at the sea' – which means harnessing good energy to the building.*

The **Repulse Bay Plaza** in the same complex offers an array of shops, boutiques, spas, banks and restaurants. The choice is not as great as in downtown Hong Kong, but is convenient for the residents and visitors staying in this area. To get to Repulse Bay, take bus 6, 6A, 6X or 260 from Exchange Square Bus Terminal.

STANLEY ★★★

One of Hong Kong's most popular destinations, Stanley is located southeast of Repulse Bay on a peninsula with a scenic promenade. It is an interesting place if you want to get away from the city and it's worth spending a day here, browsing through the market and the village. It would make an ideal combination with a visit to Repulse Bay nearby – relax on the beach after a day strolling round Stanley and check out the sunset.

Stanley Bay was once the domain of pirates and legend has it that the notorious pirate at the time, **Cheung Po Tsai** (see panel, page 47), used to rule the roost here. His hideout was a cave near the present-day **Tin Hau Temple**, which he built in 1767, believed to be one of the oldest temples in Hong Kong. The cave was filled up in the early 1950s.

Local people still refer to this area as Chek Chue or 'Bandit's House' in the Hakka dialect. Another version tells that it was named after the red flowers of the cotton trees which grew in abundance at the time and the name means 'Red Pillar' in the local dialect. When the British came, they named it Stanley, after **Lord Stanley**, the 14th Earl of Derby, who was the State Secretary for War and the Colonies between 1841 and 1845. He landed here on his official visit to Hong Kong.

Stanley has a very relaxed atmosphere, with beaches at Stanley Main Beach and St Stephen's Beach, while the waterfront in Stanley Main Street in the village is dotted with restaurants and bars. Stanley Main Beach is popular with windsurfers and plays host to the annual **Stanley Dragon Boat Race** (see panel, page 43). Most visitors go to Stanley to browse through the renowned Stanley Market to pick up bargains, gifts and souvenirs.

Stanley Market ***

There are several well-known markets in Kowloon and Hong Kong Island, but the most enjoyable to visit is Stanley Market. It has a more relaxed atmosphere with a seaside ambience. The plethora of market stalls are housed in narrow lanes covered by Perspex roofing throughout to allow the light in but yet be sheltered from the sun, as it operates only in the daytime (10:30–18:30). It is a good place to shop for **silk goods** especially traditional Chinese jackets, other silk garments, tablecloths, place mats and table runners. Other great bargains here are T-shirts with logos, paintings, lacquer ware, souvenirs, handbags, fashion accessories and all sorts of Oriental bric-a-brac – great for gifts. The prices in this market are generally lower than at the markets downtown. As in most markets, you're expected to haggle over the prices and you could walk away with great bargains. There are small eateries and stalls around the market for refreshment.

Murray House **

Dominating the landscape along the shore of Stanley Bay, Murray House stands in Stanley Plaza (which also has a retail complex with shops and a small park). It was designed and built in 1844 by Major Aldrich and Lieutenant Collinson of the British Royal Engineers as barracks for the British army in Central. First known as the Officers' Mess, it was later called Murray House after **Sir George Murray**, the Master-General of the Ordinance, a

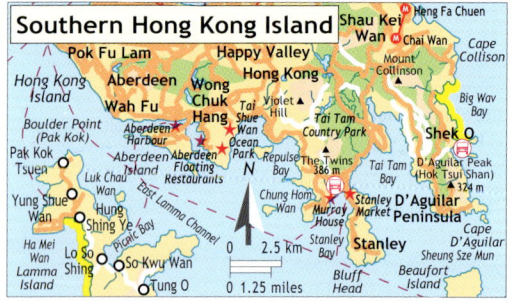

high-ranking post in the British army. During the Japanese occupation (which lasted 44 months), it was used as a command centre by the Japanese military police who tortured and executed prisoners here. As a result, it was believed to be haunted and the government twice ordered it to be officially exorcized when it was being used as offices. It was dismantled in 1982 to make way for the new Bank of China and the remains of the buildings were kept in storage for many years before being relocated and resurrected in Stanley in 1998 and reopened to the public in 1999. The building was built in a colonnaded Classical architectural style with very robust stone walls, enhanced by rows of Doric and Ionic columns on the upper floors, surrounded by verandas to allow ventilation in a subtropical climate. The ground floor houses the **Hong Kong Maritime Museum** and on the upper floors are restaurants and a café.

The Hong Kong Maritime Museum *

Housed on the ground floor of Murray House, this museum demonstrates how China, Asia and the West have contributed to the development of boats and ships in maritime exploration, trade and warfare. It pays particular attention to maritime development along the South China coast and the emergence of Hong Kong as a major trading post and international maritime centre. The Ancient and Modern galleries, with interactive maritime and seafaring games and dynamic displays, are an educational and entertaining experience for maritime enthusiasts. In front of the museum are some free-standing Ionic and Doric columns reminiscent of an ancient ruin in Greece.

Further down the seafront is **Blake Pier**, another colonial relic. It was originally a ferry pier in Central, named after **Sir Henry Arthur Blake**, the 12th governor of Hong Kong. It had to be relocated when the pier area in Central was reclaimed. It was relocated to Stanley to complement the museum. It is a good vantage point from which to enjoy the seascape in the Stanley area. Opening hours are Tue–Sun and public holidays 10:00–18:00; closed Mon and the first two days of Chinese New Year.

To get to Stanley from Central, take same bus service as to Repulse Bay (see page 45). From Causeway Bay, go to Causeway Bay MTR (Exit B) and take green minibus No. 40 from Tang Lung Street near Times Square.

CHEUNG PO TSAI, PIRATE OF THE SOUTH CHINA SEA

Cheung Po Tsai was a notorious Chinese pirate who terrorized the coastal waters of Guangdong and Hong Kong in the 19th century. He was a fisherman's son from Jiangmen in the Guangdong Province in China. It is said that when he was 15 he was kidnapped by a local pirate named Cheng I and his wife but was later adopted by them. After the death of Cheng I, Cheung Po Tsai married his adopted mother and took over the piracy business. He became a powerful and fearsome pirate and reputedly had an army of 50,000 marauders and a fleet of 600 ships. He is known to have set up bases in Stanley and Cheung Chau and is believed to have hidden his treasures in a cave on the island which today is a tourist attraction. He built temples dedicated to Tin Hau – the Protector of Seafarers and Fishermen – in Stanley, Cheung Chau and Ma Wan. After years of piracy, he gave himself up to the Qing government under the reign of Emperor Daoguang. Capitalizing on his vast experience of the sea, he was reputedly made a captain in the imperial navy. After a spell in the navy, he became a government official till the end of his life. The character of the Chinese pirate Sao Feng in the Hollywood movie *The Pirates of Caribbean: At World's End* is supposed to have been inspired by Cheung Po Tsai.

Hong Kong Island at a Glance

GETTING AROUND

The Central and Western districts are served by **MTR trains** (see page 124), with stations at Sheung Wan for the Western District, Central for Central District, and Hong Kong MTR for the Airport Express. Wan Chai and Causeway Bay have their own MTR stations. The city is well served by **public buses**, with a terminus at Exchange Square (Hong Kong MTR Exit D), and taxis. The **Star Ferry** (see panel, page 31) operates from Central Pier to Tsim Sha Tsui and Hung Hom. Adult fare is HK$2.20 for the upper deck and the crossing takes about 5–10 minutes, leaving at 8-minute intervals. There is also a Star Ferry to Kowloon; the terminal is at Wan Chai next to the Hong Kong Convention and Exhibition Centre. **Trams** operate the length of the northern coast, with termini at Kennedy Town, Whitty Street, Western Market, Causeway Bay, Happy Valley, North Point and Shau Kei Wan. The flat fare is HK$2 for adults and HK$1 for children and senior citizens; tel: 852 2548 7102, www.hktramways.com The **Peak Tram** operates daily from 07:00 to midnight at 10–15-minute intervals. The Peak Tram Sky Pass (including a visit to Peak Tower Sky Terrace) costs HK$48 for adults, HK$23 for children and senior citizens. Peak Tram (to Peak Tower only) is HK$33 for adults, HK$15 for

children and senior citizens; tel: 852 2522 0922, www.thepeak.com.hk

WHERE TO STAY

LUXURY

All luxury hotels in Hong Kong are world-class standard and feature all mod cons, Internet access, business centres, conference and banqueting facilities, spa, gym, pools, airport shuttle and all contemporary amenities of the highest standard.

Four Seasons Hotel Hong Kong, 8 Finance Street, Central, tel: 852 3196 8888, www.fourseasons.com/hongkong Luxury chain hotel, part of the prestigious ifc Mall, with unobstructed view of Victoria Harbour. The 399 rooms and 54 suites are all luxuriously designed to the signature flair of Four Seasons. Michelin-star award-winning restaurants are Lung King Heen and Caprice. Near Star Ferry and Hong Kong Station. **Island Shangri-La Hong Kong**, Pacific Place, Supreme Court Road, Central, tel: 852 2877 3838, www.shangri-la.com In prime location in Central on top of Pacific Place shopping and entertainment complex. World-class luxury hotel with 531 spacious rooms and 34 suites designed in 'Asian-accented European furnishings' with view of the city, the Peak and Victoria Harbour. Outlets include Michelin-star

award-winning restaurants Summer Palace and Petrus. **Mandarin Oriental**, 5 Connaught Road, Central, tel: 852 2522 0111, www.mandarin oriental.com/hongkong An established brand name synonymous with Hong Kong since 1963, located by the harbour within easy reach of major business and shopping centres in Central, with 502 rooms and suites designed with contemporary luxury. **Renaissance Harbour View Hotel**, 1 Harbour Road, Wan Chai, tel: 852 2802 8888, www.renaissancehotels.com/HKGHV Adjacent to the Hong Kong Convention and Exhibition Centre, commanding a panoramic view of Victoria Harbour in the heart of the business district and near Star Ferry to Kowloon, with 809 rooms and 53 suites including all mod cons. **Grand Hyatt**, 1 Harbour Road, Wan Chai, tel: 852 2588 1234, www.hongkong.grand.hyatt.com Interconnected to the Hong Kong Convention and Exhibition Centre, in the centre of the business district with 549 rooms and suites fitted with floor-to-ceiling windows for panoramic view of Victoria Harbour and city.

MID-RANGE

Metropark Hotel Wan Chai, 41–49 Hennessy Road, Wan Chai, tel: 852 2861 1166, www.metroparkhotels.com

Hong Kong Island at a Glance

Positioned right in the bustling heart of Wan Chai, near Wan Chai MTR, this 173-room small hotel was recently renovated, and some rooms were designed especially for female travellers, with ladies' amenities.

The Charterhouse, 209–219 Wan Chai Road, Wan Chai, tel: 852 2833 5566, www.charterhouse.com Juxtaposed between Wan Chai and Causeway within easy reach of both districts for shopping and sightseeing, The Charterhouse has 294 well-appointed rooms including four suites.

Excelsior, 281 Gloucester Road, Causeway Bay, tel: 852 2894 8888, www.excelsiorhongkong.com Part of the Mandarin Oriental Hotel Group, the Excelsior has a superb location in Causeway Bay right on the waterfront overlooking a marina and close to the Noon Day Gun. There are 864 rooms and 22 suites. Times Square and the MTR are just round the corner, affording very easy access to the business and entertainment district.

Regal Hongkong Hotel, 88 Yee Wo Street, Causeway Bay, tel: 852 2890 6633, www.regalhongkong.com Situated near Victoria Park in Causeway Bay, close to the MTR and Times Square and shopping districts, the hotel has 475 rooms including 30

suites all designed with a Baroque touch.

The Park Lane Hong Kong, 310 Gloucester Road, Causeway Bay, tel: 852 2293 8888, www.parkland.com.hk Located in the heart of Causeway within walking distance of Times Square and shopping malls, Victoria Park and MTR, there are 810 rooms including 34 suites.

LOWER MID-RANGE / BOUTIQUE
Lan Kwai Fong Hotel, No. 3 Kau U Fong, Central, tel: 852 3650 0000, www.lankwai fong.com.hk A design-led boutique hotel in the heart of Central with stylish contemporary decor accented with Oriental charm. There are 158 rooms and suites, each with its own special touches.

Central Park Hotel, 263 Hollywood Road, Central, tel: 852 2850 8899. This is a hip boutique hotel located in an interesting part of the city in Hollywood Road surrounded by historic sites and antiques shops. Refreshing colour scheme in green and white, with 142 rooms including six executive suites.

Bishop Lei International House, 4 Robinson Road, Mid-Levels, Central, tel: 852 2868 0828, www.bishoplei htl.com.hk Owned and operated by the Catholic Diocese of Hong Kong, this modest and comfortable hotel is located in a quieter part of Central away from the bustle

of the financial and shopping centre but within walkable distance. There are 219 functional rooms, one food outlet and a pool.

Cosmo Hotel, 375–377 Queen's Road East, Wan Chai, tel: 852 3552 8388, www.cosmohotel.com.hk Chic upbeat hotel situated between Wan Chai and Causeway with hi-tech facilities and 142 colour-coded rooms and suites. Best rates offered if booked online.

The Wesley Hong Kong, 22 Hennessy Road, Wan Chai, tel: 852 2866 6688, tw@hanglung.com www.hanglung.com Located in the centre of Wan Chai in the vicinity of Pacific Place shopping mall and Queensway Plaza and entertainment centres, the hotel has 250 functional rooms.

Holiday Inn Express Causeway Bay Hong Kong, 33 Sharp Street East, Causeway Bay, tel: 852 3558 6688, rsvn@expresscw.com www.expressbyholidayinn. com.cn Superbly located next to Times Square and the MTR, a new functional no-frills 282-room hotel with basic but adequate facilities and amenities. There is no porter service (trolleys are provided for self-service) but the hotel compensates with free breakfast and free broadband Internet included in the rates. Best rates guaranteed for online booking.

Hong Kong Island at a Glance

CHINESE CUISINE

Lung King Heen, Four Seasons Hotel Hong Kong, 8 Finance Street, Central, tel: 852 3196 8888. This three-star Michelin award-winning contemporary Cantonese restaurant specializes in dim sum, seafood and Chinese *haute cuisine*, served in a chic ambience.

Maxim's Palace, Low Block, City Hall, Connaught Road, Central, tel: 852 2526 9931 (enquiries only, no reservations allowed). For a quintessentially Hong Kong *yum cha* experience, this massive lively restaurant, famous for its vast variety of dim sum served on trolleys, is the best option. Opens daily from 11:00–15:00.

Chiu Chow Garden, Shop 202, 2/F, Hutchinson House, Central, tel: 852 2536 0833. This is a modern restaurant serving Chiu Chow cuisine with wagyu beef cheek pot pie braised in red wine as one of its signature dishes. Opens 11:30–15:00 (lunch), 18:00–23:30 (dinner),

Yung Kee, 32–40 Wellington Street, Central, tel: 852 2522 1624. A one-star Michelin award-winning outlet, this is one of Hong Kong's finest Cantonese restaurants and it is famous for its roast goose and other fine Cantonese dishes. Opens daily from 11:00–23:30.

Bo Innovation, UG/F, Ice House, 32–38 Ice House Street, Central, tel: 852 2850 8371. Owned by celebrity chef Alvin Leung, this restaurant is famous for its innovative Chinese fusion cuisine that takes modern gastronomy to a new dimension (e.g. Chinese chicken sausage ice cream and oyster tofu). Opens 12:00–15:00 (lunch), 19:00 to midnight (dinner).

Yee Tung Heen, The Excelsior Hong Kong, 281 Gloucester Road, Causeway Bay, tel: 852 2837 6790. Authentic Cantonese, Sichuan and Hunan cuisines are served at this restaurant, and great dim sum too, with harbour view. Opens Mon–Sat 11:30–14:30, Sun 10:30–15:00 (lunch); daily 18:00–22:30 (dinner).

Tai Ping Koon Restaurant, 6 Pak Sha Road, Causeway Bay, tel: 852 2576 9161. An established East-West restaurant favoured by local celebrities for its speciality dishes such as Swiss sauce chicken wings, roast pigeon and the beef hor fun noodle dish. Opens from 11:00 to midnight.

STREET NOSH

Informal restaurants serving Hong Kong's favourite street food are popular at breakfast and lunch times.

Keung Kee Restaurant, 9–17 Tin Lok Lane, Wan Chai, tel: 852 2574 5991. This restaurant is well known for its delicious roast meat, notably roast goose and barbeque pork. Opens from 07:00 to midnight.

Wing Kee, G/F 43 Jardine's Bazaar, Central, tel: 852 2576 3688. With a selection of noodle dishes served from the 'Cart Noodles' as well as *congee*, this is a great place to sample typical local street fare. Opens 11:00–22:30.

Ho Hung Kee Congee & Noodle Wonton Shop, G/F, 2 Sharp Street East, Causeway Bay, tel: 852 2577 6558. This establishment is renowned for its wide variety of congee (savoury rice porridge) and noodle dishes. Opens 11:30–23:00.

Tai Cheong Bakery, 32 Lyndhurst Terrace, Central, tel: 852 2854 3810. This bakery is well known for its delicious egg tarts, Hong Kong's signature pastry – once bitten, forever smitten. Makes great take away for tea time or snacking. Opens Mon–Sat 07:30–20:30, Sun and public holidays 08:30–19:30.

INTERNATIONAL & WESTERN

The Peak Lookout, 121 Peak Road, the Peak, tel: 852 2849 1000. This restaurant serves eclectic cuisine – with Asian, Indian, Italian and a grill selection – in a great location by the Peak Tower. Opens from 10:00–15:00 (lunch) and 15:00 to midnight (dinner).

Hong Kong Island at a Glance

TOTT'S, 34/F, The Excelsior Hong Kong, Causeway Bay, tel: 852 2837 6786. Enjoy dining 'in the clouds' on the 34th floor of the Excelsior hotel, with a spectacular view of Victoria Harbour. This restaurant features contemporary fusion cuisine. Opens Mon–Fri 12:00–15:00, Sun 11:30–15:00 (lunch), Mon–Sat 18:00–23:00, Sun 18:30–22:00 (dinner).

Jimmy's Kitchen, G/F, South China Building, 1–3 Wyndham Street, Central, tel: 852 2526 5293. Good old-fashioned classic Western fare in traditional British pub ambience. Opens 12:00–15:00 (lunch), 18:00–23:00 (dinner).

Rei Sushi, Shop 1103, Level 1, ifc Mall, 8 Finance Street, Central, tel: 852 3188 1900. Classic Japanese cuisine like sushi, sashimi and house specialities served in an informal setting. This restaurant opens 11:30–15:00 (lunch), 18:00–23:00 (dinner).

Simply Thai, Shop 1104, 11/F, Food Forum, Times Square, Causeway Bay, tel: 852 2506 1212. A restaurant featuring classic and modern Thai cuisines amid elegant decor. Opens 11:30–15:00 (lunch), 17:30–22:30 (dinner).

Wooloomooloo, G/F & 1/F, ONFEM Tower, 29 Wyndham Street, Central, tel: 852 2894 8010. No-nonsense Australian menu offers hearty man-size steaks and seafood selection in 'Down Under' outback theme with open kitchen as centrepiece. Opens 11:45–14:30 (lunch) and 17:30–23:00 (dinner).

SHOPPING

The Central District is one mega shopping mall and more up-market than Kowloon side. Popular malls are the Landmark Centre, Princes Building, Pacific Place, Swire House and ifc Mall at Finance Street. For antiques and handicrafts, Hollywood Road and Upper Lascar Row have the most choice. Causeway Bay is another great place to shop, and Times Square is the main shopping precinct.

TOURS AND EXCURSIONS

The best way to get an overview of Hong Kong in comfort and leisure is to join the many excursions on offer by tour companies with English-speaking guides in comfortable air-conditioned buses.

Travel Asia (HK) Ltd, 17/F, 10 Knutsford Terrace, Tsim Sha Tsui, Kowloon, tel: 852 2721 0222, info@travelasia.com.hk www.travelasia.com.hk One of Hong Kong's leading tour operators which also operates tours to Macau and China.

Splendid Tours, Sheraton Hong Kong Hotel & Tower, The Lobby, 2nd Level, Tsim Sha Tsui, Kowloon, tel: 852 2316 2151, info@splendid.hk www.splendid.hk An established tour company who has tour desks in major hotels in Kowloon and Hong Kong.

Big Bus Company, The Big Bus Company (HK) Ltd, Unit 501, 5th Floor, No. 1 Minden Avenue, Tsim Sha Tsui, Kowloon, tel: 852 2723 2108, infohk@bigbustours.com www.bigbustours.com Sightseeing from open-top buses with digitally recorded commentary.

Star Ferry's Harbour Tour, tel: 852 2118 6201/6202, harbourtour@starferry.com.hk www.starferry.com.hk/harbourtour An hour-long cruise around Victoria Harbour.

Tram Cars: A fascinating way to see the sights of northern Hong Kong is to travel on the tram cars from Central eastwards to Shau Kei Wan Terminus, taking in all the sights in between, or getting off in Wan Chai and Causeway Bay to explore the areas before catching another tram to continue the journey. There is a flat fare of HK\$2 for adults and HK\$1 for children and senior citizens. Note: Board from the back and exit through the front – you pay as you exit.

EMERGENCY NUMBERS

Police, Fire and Ambulance, tel: 999
Police Hotline, tel: 852 2527 7177.

4
Kowloon and Beyond

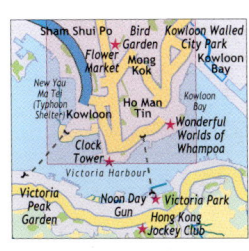

While Hong Kong Island shows its British colonial legacy and is hard-wired to commerce with its sophisticated swanky skyscrapers, Kowloon is the heart of the country's Chinese heritage, uncompromising in its Eastern culture and lifestyle. Located across the harbour north of the island, covering 47km² (18 sq miles), it is densely populated and less glamorous with a much lower skyline due to its close proximity to Kai Tak, the old airport of Hong Kong. The area was largely developed in the early 20th century following the opening of the Kowloon-Canton Railway and Kowloon Wharf. Today Kowloon is a pulsating metropolis and offers a cornucopia of tourist attractions, especially in its downtown areas Tsim Sha Tsui, Yua Mai Tei and Mong Kok, all served by MTR and buses along Nathan Road.

Tsim Sha Tsui

Tsim Sha Tsui, or 'Deep Sandy Water', is the southernmost part of the Kowloon Peninsula and the name probably refers to the harbour. It reflects a different face of Hong Kong. It is more crowded than Hong Kong Island, heaves with people and traffic, and its tone is more ethnic and rustic. But in recent years it has also become a cultural centre with museums and art galleries.

Nathan Road ***

Known as the Golden Mile, Nathan Road is the main thoroughfare in downtown Kowloon, stretching from Salisbury Road in Tsim Sha Tsui in the south by the

---

DON'T MISS

*** Nathan Road: lively shopping and entertainment.
*** Harbour Front: Avenue of Stars, Symphony of Lights, harbour cruise on *Duk Ling*.
*** The Peninsula: afternoon tea, charming ambience.
*** Sik Sik Yuen Wong Tai Sin Temple: spiritual place.
*** Markets: bargains galore, lively atmosphere.
** Bird Garden and Flower Market: in Kowloon.
** Kowloon Park and **Kowloon Walled City Park:** tranquil oasis of calm.
** Lei Yue Mun Seafood Bazaar: seafood feast.

Opposite: *Nathan Road by night is a riot of colour.*

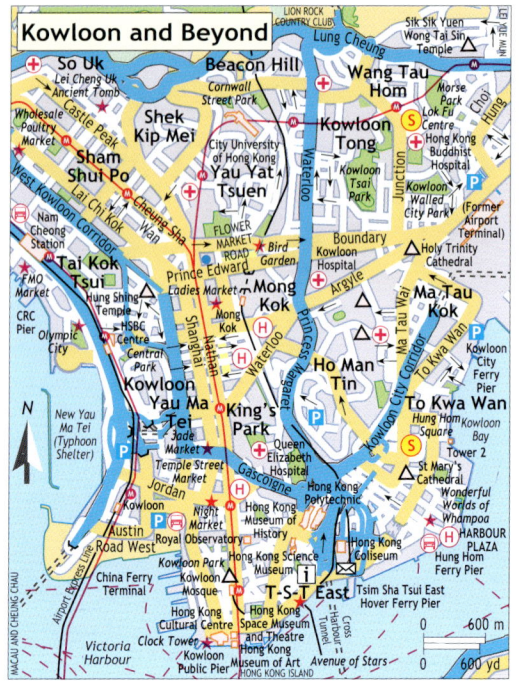

harbour to Boundary Street in Mong Kok in the north. It is the busiest road in Hong Kong – with wall to wall with shopping complexes, markets, restaurants, entertainment centres and bars centred on the main road and branching off along the side streets. At night it is ablaze with thousands of neon lights beaming out commercial messages and advertisements to consumers.

Adjacent to Haiphong Road is **Kowloon Park**, an oasis of calm and tranquillity among the hustle and bustle of Nathan Road. It is a lovely park with a shrubbery maze, rose garden, a pavilion and turtle ponds. It is a favourite place for the locals to do t'ai chi and Chinese-style alfresco line dancing among the bauhinia trees early in the morning. By the park is the **Kowloon Mosque and Islamic Centre**, one of four main mosques in Hong Kong. It is conspicuous among the modern offices and shops, with its gleaming white marble façades adorned with four minarets, one on each corner of the mosque, and topped by a white dome on its upper terrace. On Fridays it is very busy with worshippers, jostling among the shoppers, tourists and office workers.

Nathan Road was the first road to be built in Kowloon (in 1861) and was named after **Sir Matthew Nathan**, 13th Governor of Hong Kong. It is a lively place to visit and absorb the excitement of this thriving Chinese domain.

The Harbour Front ★★★

The waterfront runs along Salisbury Road and has been upgraded to include Hong Kong Cultural Centre, Hong Kong Space Museum and Theatre, Hong Kong Museum of Art and its latest attraction, the Avenue of Stars along the Tsim Sha Tsui promenade. This is also the vantage point from which to watch the nightly Symphony of Lights. The Star Ferry Pier is located here and nearby is the **Clock Tower**, a landmark monument of Hong Kong. It is all that is left of the former Kowloon Station on the Kowloon-Canton Railway built in 1915. Standing at 44m (144ft) high and crowned by a 7m-tall (23ft) lightning rod, its four façades are installed with a clock face each. The clocks began operating on 22 March 1921 and have been ticking ever since, except during the Japanese occupation in World War II. Just round the corner on the western side of the peninsula is the Hong Kong China Ferry Terminal, Harbour City Ocean Terminal and Harbour City Ocean Centre – a large complex of hotels, offices, restaurants and shopping malls mainly retailing in designer labels. The most prominent building along Salisbury Road is the renowned Peninsula Hotel, the most iconic and historic hotel in Hong Kong (see panel, this page).

Hong Kong Space Museum and Theatre ★★

The museum is situated next to the Cultural Centre (see panel, page 57). It was opened in October 1980 with a mission to showcase space science and astronomy for educational and entertainment purposes through its exhibition and interactive experiences. The 8000m^2 (86,111-sq-ft) modern building with an imposing giant dome is one of the most renowned edifices by the harbour front. It is divided into two wings. The **East Wing** with the dome is the Stanley Ho Space Theatre, Hall of Space Science, workshops and offices. The Space Theatre has a hemispherical projection dome with a diameter of 23m (75ft). It boasts the first OMNIMAX film projector in the eastern hemisphere and is also the first museum in the world to possess a fully automatic

THE PENINSULA HONG KONG

Dubbed affectionately as 'The Pen', the grande dame of Hong Kong was designed to be the 'finest hotel east of Suez' since its grand opening on 11 December 1928. Owned by the Kadoorie family, the Peninsula was the 'jewel in the family crown' and the vision and confidence of the two founder Kadoorie brothers – Ellis and Elly – to open such a grand hotel in a turbulent political climate at the time was not misplaced. With the advent of luxury ocean liners calling at Victoria Harbour and the opening of the Kowloon-Canton Railway line, international travellers were calling at Hong Kong in droves and 'The Pen' was their first choice of accommodation. Today, with its original building upgraded and a new 30-storey tower added in 1994, it still reigns supreme. The traditional Afternoon Tea Dance has been revived and is held on the first Sunday of every month from Mar–Dec in the grand lobby where guests are taken back in time with Peninsula Swing's own big-band repertoire. The China Clipper on the 30th floor serves as a helipad and provides a unique venue for small private functions with a commanding view of the harbour. A fleet of 14 custom-made Rolls-Royce Extended Wheelbase Phantoms is available for the exclusive use of guests.

control system. Each year it produces two multimedia planetarium shows. The **West Wing** houses the Hall of Astronomy, Lecture Hall, gift shops and offices. For those interested in experiencing a virtual exploration of the final frontier in outer space, it is worth spending half a day there, and the Stanley Ho Space Theatre is both entertaining and awe-inspiring. Located at 10 Salisbury Road, Tsim Sha Tsui, Kowloon, it is open Mon, Wed, Thu and Fri 13:00–21:00 (closed Tue except public holidays); Sat, Sun and public holidays 10:00–21:00 (closed on the first two days of Chinese New Year). Children under three years old will not be admitted to the theatre. For Stanley Ho Space Theatre show times, tel: 852 2721 0226.

Hong Kong Museum of Art **

Within a stone's throw of the Space Museum is the Hong Kong Museum of Art. It has an extensive collection of oil paintings, drawings and etchings as well as lithographs of old Hong Kong displayed over seven exhibition galleries. Chinese antiquities, Chinese fine arts, historical pictures and contemporary Hong Kong art are exhibited in four galleries, while two other galleries house special exhibitions of works of art by international artists to keep Hong Kong up to date with global art trends. The seventh gallery holds a special exhibition of the famous **Xubaizhai Collection** of Chinese paintings and calligraphy from the 5th century to 20th century, including major masters from the Ming and Qing dynasties, donated by Mr Low Chuk Tiew, a renowned local collector. Located at 10 Salisbury Road, Tsim Sha Tsui, Kowloon, the museum is open Fri and Sun–Wed 10:00–18:00, Sat 10:00–20:00, closed Thu (except public holidays). It is open on public holidays except the first two days of Chinese New Year. To get there (and also to the Hong Kong Space Museum and Theatre and the Hong Kong Cultural Centre), follow the signs from Tsim Sha Tsui MTR Exit E and walk to the museum through the subway. It is five minutes from the Star Ferry.

Avenue of Stars ★★★

Located right on the water's edge along the Tsim Sha Tsui promenade is the Avenue of Stars, dedicated to the Hong Kong movie industry. It is a tribute to the stars of the silver screen and also the star-makers. There are plaques and hand prints of famous stars in the Chinese movie industry, including internationally well-known Chinese stars like Jackie Chan, Michelle Yeoh, Chow Yun Fat and Jet Li. Bronze sculptures of movie directors and camera men in action create a movie-set scene along the promenade. Avenue of Stars also pays special homage to the legendary **Bruce Lee**, the late Hong Kong kung fu megastar of the 70s who died in his prime (*see* panel, page 56). A life-like giant statue of the movie icon dominates the avenue. To his legions of fans it is a favourite place for a photo opportunity. The promenade is a great place to stroll along, admiring the harbour view, and a vantage point from which to watch the Symphony of Lights from Kowloon side. To get there, from Tsim Sha Tsui MTR Exit F, take the pedestrian subway tunnel to Tsim Sha Tsui East KCR station Exit J and follow the signs. It is also accessible from Hong Kong Space Museum and Hong Kong Museum of Art (about three minutes' walk), Exit E at Tsim Sha Tsui MTR.

Hong Kong Museum of History ★★

The Hong Kong Museum of History is located in Tsim Sha Tsui East, about 20 minutes' walk from the Hong Kong Space Museum area. The museum was established in 1975 to preserve and promote the historical and cultural heritage of Hong Kong. The permanent exhibition of '**The Hong Kong Story**', covering an area of 7000m² (75,347 sq ft) over eight galleries, is both fas-

Below: *Bronze statue of Bruce Lee, in his famous iconic kung fu pose, on the Avenue of Stars in Tsim Sha Tsui.*

Above: *The Hong Kong Science Museum offers visitors interactive exhibits to make science fun, educational and entertaining.*

cinating and educational. It showcases the natural environment of the region starting from 400 million years ago in the Devonian period progressing to its early human settlement, folk culture, and the historical development of Hong Kong from the Han to the Qing dynasties right up to the handover of Hong Kong in 1997. The 4000 exhibits are displayed in 750 graphic panels, numerous dioramas and multimedia programmes enhanced by special audiovisual and lighting effects to project a life-like and entertaining exhibition. It is open Mon and Wed–Sat 10:00–18:00, Sun and public holidays 10:00–19:00; closed Tue and the first two days of Chinese New Year. Admission is free on Wed. There are regular guided tours for 'The Hong Kong Story' by museum guides; check times at the museum. It is located at 100 Chatham Road South, Tsim Sha Tsui East, Kowloon. To get there, from Tsim Sha Tsui MTR walk towards Tsim Sha Tsui East for about 20 minutes.

The Hong Kong Science Museum **

Adjacent to the history museum, the Hong Kong Science Museum was opened in 1991, with 6500m² (69,965 sq ft) of exhibition spaces housing 500 exhibits, of which 70% are interactive and suitable for all ages. It aims to make science fun, entertaining and educational by popularizing science to the public and supporting science education in schools. Visitors are able to participate in the science experience and have fun at the same time. Its showpiece exhibit is the **Energy Machine**, the largest of its kind in the world, standing at 22m (72ft) high and occupying four storeys of space in a prominent position in the centre of the exhibition halls. It demonstrates the movement of energy. When set in motion, a continuous stream of balls made of synthetic fibre measuring 19cm (7.5in) in diameter will roll like a roller coaster from one tower to another tower linked by a connecting gallery, producing clanging sounds and visual effects. The balls take 1.5 minutes to complete the circuit of 1.6km (1 mile) of tracks. It is the highlight of the museum and large crowds gather when the machine is in action.

The museum is open Mon, Tue, Wed and Fri 13:00–21:00, Sat, Sun and public holidays 10:00–21:00; closed Thu (except public holidays) and the first two days of Chinese New Year. Free admission on Wed. It is located at 2 Science Museum Road, Tsim Sha Tsui East, Kowloon. To get there, from Tsim Sha Tsui MTR walk towards Tsim Sha Tsui East for about 20 minutes.

YAU MA TEI AND MONG KOK

Further north on Nathan Road are Yau Ma Tei and Mong Kok, the heart of the Kowloon Peninsula. Mong Kok has one of the highest population densities in the world. This is the heartland of the Chinese community, without the gloss and glitz of Hong Kong Island. Here the cacophony and pulsating rhythm of life in the typically Chinese enclaves resonate through the crowded narrow streets and cramped residential areas. You can immerse yourself in the local ambience, jostling with the heaving mass and browsing through the many shops and markets, with bargains galore, hawking traditional Chinese wares, clothing, electronic goods and other local paraphernalia. Hawkers' stalls at street corners serve up local delicacies and fast food. There are some interesting places around here to step into the world of traditional Hong Kong.

Temple Street Market ★★★

Also known as 'Men's Street', this is one of the most renowned markets in Kowloon and very popular with tourists eager to find bargains among its many stalls. The market was named after a temple dedicated to Tin

7-ELEVEN: A CONVENIENT FRIEND

The ubiquitous 7-Eleven convenience stores have been in Hong Kong since 1981, with (aptly) 711 stores in the country. They offer very useful services, from selling and topping up sim cards for mobile phones and Octopus cards to selling food and drinks, toiletries and other travellers' essentials. They have been sprouting up everywhere in the city, providing convenient services for visitors and locals. Look out for the green, white and red '7' sign. The store was founded in 1927 in Dallas, Texas, and was originally known as Tote'm store but was renamed 7-Eleven in 1946 after its opening hours. Today it is the largest convenience retail chain in the world, with franchises globally.

Above: *Ladies' Market in Mong Kok is a bustling and colourful market.*

Hau, the Goddess of the Sea, which was built in the area. Like all markets here, it offers a variety of inexpensive clothing and items especially for men, though there are plenty of goods for the ladies too. Fortune-tellers – and sometimes even impromptu Cantonese opera performances – add to the trading carnival at the far end of the street. Behind the market stalls are shops competing with the market in selling discount goods. Haggling is the order of the day. The market opens at 16:00 to midnight daily. To get there, go to Jordan MTR Exit A. Turn right at Jordan Road, and walk three blocks to Temple Street.

Jade Market and Jade Street **

For jade lovers, the Jade Market is a great place to visit, with 400 stalls festooned with everything jade – from trinkets, necklaces and bangles to jade artefacts and ornaments. Everything comes in different colours, shapes and designs. Close by is Jade Street, located in Canton Road between Kansu Street and Jordan Road, selling more jade. Unless you are an expert on jade, be wary of buying expensive pieces as it would be difficult to authenticate the quality of the jade. But for a bit of fun to buy jade jewellery and ornaments for gifts, it is quite interesting to browse through the stalls. Bargain and great pieces can be found if you are patient enough to sieve through the mountains of jade products. Jade Market opens from 10:00–17:00 daily while Jade Street opens 10:30–14:30. To get there, walk from Yau Ma Tei MTR Exit C towards Kansu Street.

Ladies' Market ***

Twinned with Temple Street Market, and just as famous, is Ladies' Market, further up Nathan Road in Mong Kok, in Tung Choi Street. Despite its name, it is not confined to women's goods though originally it was set up to be. It is a great place to soak up the frenzied atmosphere, jostling through the crowd and seeking out bargains of fashion items and attire for both men and women, luggage, handbags, children's clothing and toys, household goods and all sorts of inexpensive tacky paraphernalia – the sort of thing that is the mainstay of street markets. It opens daily from noon till 23:30 and gets especially busy after dark, with office workers and locals joining in the throngs of tourists. As in all crowded places, beware of pickpockets. To get there, walk the short distance from Mong Kok MTR Exit E2 (Nelson Street exit) to Tung Choi Street (signposted to Ladies' Market).

Bird Garden and Flower Market **

The Bird Garden and Flower Market in northern Mong Kok used to epitomize the daily life of the local residents going about their business, but they have become tourist attractions. Before heading there, it is worth walking through the many side streets off Nathan Road in Mong Kok to savour the bustling tempo of un-touristy places and street markets selling fruits, vegetables, Chinese goods and herbs purely for the locals. **Shanghai Street**, parallel to Nathan Road, is a fascinating place to explore with its old-school type of shops, like in days of yore in Hong Kong, retailing in traditional goods, elaborate Chinese wedding gowns, feng shui products, Chinese artefacts and books. It was the main business district in the area before Nathan Road assumed the role.

The **Flower Market** is a street in full bloom with retail and wholesale trade in flowers and plants. It is bursting with colours of the many varieties of flowers, including a plethora of exotic orchids from Southeast Asian countries. Of particular interest are the pitcher plants, normally grown wild in rainforests but now cultivated in nurseries and sold in hanging pots; they make an exotic and unique display in homes. Each shop along Flower Market Road is bedecked with plants and flowers in pots as well as bouquets. The area is thronged with the

Above: *The Bird Garden, with its plethora of exotic birds in cages, is a twittering alley of everything to do with birds and their accessories.*

local denizens buying greenery and flowers for their homes and gardens and haggling with the retailers.

At the top of the street is the **Bird Garden** at Yeun Po Street where the old Chinese tradition of bird-keeping is very much practised and thriving. Set in a Chinese-style garden complete with moon gates and willow trees, a narrow alley by the side of the garden is lined with bird cages containing all sorts of birds and every accessory that a bird-keeper might need. Bird cages of all shapes and sizes festoon the alleyway, while heaving masses of wriggling worms and crickets (food for pet birds) are put on display for sale by the cages. Exotic birds like macaws, parrots and budgies make up the colourful displays and the whole garden is alive with the sound of bird song. Wild sparrows flock here to feed on the crumbs from the cages of their imprisoned feathered friends, celebrating their own freedom with a chorus of warbling and squabbling for food. The caged birds appear to be well cared for, though they would probably prefer flying free among the trees. In the heat of the afternoon, some owners spray cold water on the birds to keep them cool and clean and the birds seem to enjoy the spa treatment by spreading their wings to receive the spray. It is customary for elderly men to take their pampered birds in bamboo cages for a walk here and show off their singing talents to other bird fanciers. Sometimes there is quite a keen warbling competition among the birds. Some parrots are even taught to say greetings in Chinese to passers-by as their proud owners look on. If an encounter with the feathered kind is your cup of tea, the Bird Garden will not disappoint.

WONG TAI SIN
Sik Sik Yuen Wong Tai Sin Temple ★★★

Beyond the boundaries of Kowloon proper is one of the most famous temples in Hong Kong, the Wong Tai Sin Temple. It is often referred to with the prefix 'Sik Sik Yuen', the name of a religious organization which manages the temple. Wong Tai Sin, or 'Great Immortal Wong', is a Taoist god originally from Guangdong Province. He was immortalized and enlightened after spending 40 years as a recluse studying Taoism and learning the art of immortalization in the Jinha Mountain. In 1915, a Taoist priest called Liang Renan and his son Liang Junzhuan brought the sacred portrait of Wong Tai Sin to Hong Kong and set up a small temple in Wan Chai. Through divine guidance from Wong Tai Sin, they were advised to build a new shrine in Kowloon City. The temple was subsequently moved to its present site in 1921 and Sik Sik Yuen was formally established to look after the management of the temple. It is also a charity foundation that offers education, subsidized medical services and social services, particularly in the care of the elderly and children. **Po Chai Hall**, the medical building by the entrance, was opened in 1981, offering subsidized Chinese traditional medicine and Western medicine for the local residents and the underprivileged.

Below: *Wong Tai Sin, one of Hong Kong's most revered and famous temples, attracts hundreds of devotees each day, praying for good fortune.*

Wong Tai Sin is a very ornate temple that comprises the Main Altar, the Three Saints Temple, the Confucius Hall and the Yue Heung Shrine as the principle buildings among other subsidiary pavilions and shrines. It was built in accordance to feng shui principles, incorporating the five elements of metal, wood, water, fire and earth, represented by the

SEAFOOD AT LEI YUE MUN

At Lei Yue Mun's market stalls various sea creatures are kept alive in big tanks. Diners can select and pay for the seafood at the market stalls and then get it cooked at the restaurants by the market for a fee. The restaurants will tailor-make the recipe in accordance with the diner's wishes. It is a novel way of dining in a village atmosphere right by the city. To get there, take the green minibus 24 from Yau Tong MTR Exit A2 to Sam Ka Tsuen Ferry Pier, then follow the signs to the village; it's about a 15-minute walk, or take a taxi.

Bronze Pavilion (metal); Archive Hall (wood); Yuk Yik Fountain of seven metallic lotuses (water); Yue Heung Shrine dedicated to Buddha of the 'Lighting Lamp' (fire), and the earth wall (earth). The Good Wish Garden in the compound is designed in a traditional Chinese landscape garden style with a series of pagodas in various shapes interlinked by a zigzag corridor, a replica of the Summer Palace in Beijing. The large fish pond, linked by arched bridges overlooked by an artificial waterfall, is a picture of tranquillity in contrast to the high-rise apartments towering over the temple outside the garden wall. Wong Tai Sin is a much-revered god and the temple is famous for its fortune-telling. Hundreds of devotees come here daily to read their fortune and offer prayers and votive offerings to Wong Tai Sin, whose portrait is displayed in the Main Altar along with paintings and teachings of Buddhism, Taoism and Confucianism. They strongly believe that Wong Tai Sin has the power to grant their wishes. To get there, it is a three-minute walk to the temple from Wong Tai Sin MTR Exit B2 or B3.

KOWLOON CITY
Kowloon Walled City Park **

This area in Kowloon City was once a rough neighbourhood of high-rise slums and lawlessness known as the Kowloon Walled City. It was demolished and turned into an award-winning park in 1995, preserving the history of the former Walled City in the style of a traditional Chinese garden of the Qing Dynasty. It is a pleasant green escape in the city, with pavilions, sculptures, flower gardens and play-

Below: *Kowloon Walled City Park, once the site of a lawless walled-up slum, is now a picture of serene greenery and tranquillity.*

grounds. It also features a Qing Dynasty almshouse and the **Old South Gate**, a remnant of its history. The **Yamen**, or historical administrative building, has been restored and preserved *in situ* with two cannons, made in 1802, also surviving relics. The park has six landscaped themes: the **Garden of the Chinese Zodiac**, the **Chess Garden**, the **Mountain View Pavilion**, the **Kuixing Pavilion and Guibi Rock**, **Eight Floral Walks**, and the **Garden of Four Seasons**. The tranquillity of the park today makes it a favourite place for the local residents to relax and exercise. It opens from 06:30–23:00. To get there, take a taxi from Lok Fu MTR Exit B to the North Gate entrance on Tung Tau Tsuen Road, or take bus 1 from the Tsim Sha Tsui Star Ferry Bus Terminus and alight at Tung Tau Tsuen Road (opposite the park).

LEI YUE MUN **

The name of this fishing village, Lei Yue Mun, means 'Carp's Gate' in Chinese. It is situated by a narrow channel in the southeastern corner of the peninsula between Junk Bay and Victoria Harbour and forms the eastern gate of the harbour. The fishing village came into prominence in the 1960s when the locals discovered its renowned seafood markets and restaurants. But business was boosted after a **seafood festival** was organized in the village in 1992, with the restaurants dishing up special promotion and dishes. Since then the festival has been an annual event with a lively carnival of lion dances, gongs and drums complemented by Cantonese opera singing and a giant seafood feast.

Today, the rustic air of the village still lingers on, with fishing boats berthing by structures built on stilts over the water, but it has been modernized, sanitized and surrounded by high-rise flats. However, it still holds its position as a popular destination for seafood lovers who flock here to dine on fresh seafood – so fresh, in fact, that the items on the menu are practically still swimming in their tanks. Market stalls (*see* panel, page 64) line the seafront, selling live fish, lobsters, shellfish, squid and other sea creatures.

FORTUNE-TELLING

Throughout history the Chinese have used various divination methods to foretell their fortune. Monks and mediums in temples or feng shui masters are often consulted to do the readings. The most popular method in temples is **Kau Cim** (*see* page 25). **Palm reading** and **face reading** are also widely used by experts in those fields. Face reading interprets facial features – nose, eyes, mouth and the shape of the face – to determine a person's character and fortune. The face is divided into three phases of life: the upper part is youth, the centre represents middle age and the lower part reflects old age. For a more detailed destiny reading, the **Four Pillars of Destiny** method is often sought and feng shui masters in Hong Kong are particularly skilled in this. It involves reading a person's destiny from the natal chart: date, month, time, year and place of birth can influence their destiny. **Astrology** is often used in determining marriage compatibility. There are 12 zodiac animal signs in Chinese astrology and each animal has a perfect match or enemy; it is important to choose a partner with a compatible animal sign. Engagements have been known to be cancelled on the advice of an astrologer should a clash of zodiac signs be revealed, although the younger generation does not really heed such advice any more.

Kowloon and Beyond at a Glance

BEST TIMES TO VISIT

This is an all-year destination with a subtropical climate, but the most pleasant time of year to visit is in **November** and **December** when the weather is sunny with comfortable temperatures and very low humidity.

GETTING AROUND

Kowloon is the main hub for public transportation in the peninsula, with an extensive network of MTR **trains** (see page 124) as well as the Kowloon-Canton Railway (KCR) serving the length and breadth of the region. **Buses** supplement the rail and MTR routes and the bus services are efficient and inexpensive. The best way to travel around is to use the **Octopus Card** (see page 124), an electronic fare card that is accepted by almost all public transport. The card is especially useful as buses accept only exact fare and buying individual tickets at MTR stations involves a fair amount of queuing up at ticket machines. The Octopus Card can be purchased at MTR stations and 7-Eleven shops. **Taxis** can be hailed anywhere but more conveniently in front of hotels where they are always in service. Urban taxis are red with a white top. The **Star Ferry** Pier and Bus Terminus are both situated on Salisbury Road next to the Hong Kong Cultural Centre in Tsim Sha Tsui. There is also a Star Ferry station at Hung Hom.

WHERE TO STAY

There is a wide choice of accommodation in Kowloon and there are options to suit all budgets. All the luxury and mid-range categories are world-class and equipped with modern facilities, broadband Internet, business centres, gym and contemporary amenities. Lower-grade hotels tend to have very compact rooms but these are adequately furnished and come with basic amenities. Hotel rates fluctuate according to season and demand and are particularly high during major exhibitions in town.

LUXURY

The Peninsula, Salisbury Road, Tsim Sha Tsui, Kowloon, tel: 852 2920 2888, www.peninsula.com A famous historic landmark and iconic hotel in Hong Kong, renowned for its old-world elegance and charm and its sumptuous suites commanding a spectacular view of Victoria Harbour. It is situated by the harbour front and MTR station, near Star Ferry Pier and a two-minute walk from Nathan Road; there are 246 rooms and 54 suites.

The Mira, 118 Nathan Road, Tsim Sha Tsui, Kowloon, tel: 852 2368 1111, www.themirahotel.com An ultra-chic design-led lifestyle hotel with indulgent comfort and wired up with hi-tech facilities. It boasts a superb location in the heart of Tsim Sha Tsui, conveniently situated by the MTR and Kowloon Park.

The Sheraton Hong Kong Hotel & Towers, 20 Nathan Road, Tsim Sha Tsui, Kowloon, tel: 852 2369 1111, www.sheraton.com/hongkong A world-class hotel by the harbour front within the Golden Mile precinct of Nathan Road and by the MTR station and near Star Ferry Pier. It has 782 rooms and suites.

Kowloon Shangri-La, 64 Mody Road, Tsim Sha Tsui East, Kowloon, tel: 852 2721 2111, www.shangri-la.com Ideally located in the commercial and shopping area of Tsim Sha Tsui East, overlooking Victoria Harbour. With 700 rooms and suites, it has some of the most spacious rooms in town.

InterContinental Hong Kong, 18 Salisbury Road, Tsim Sha Tsui, Kowloon, tel: 852 2721 1211, www.hongkong-ic.intercontinental.com Located right on the waterfront with an unrivalled view of Victoria Harbour, this hotel is near Star Ferry Pier, MTR and the shopping area of Nathan Road. It has 495 rooms and suites.

Renaissance Kowloon Hotel, 22 Salisbury Road, Tsim Sha Tsui, Kowloon, tel: 852 2369 4111, www.renaissancehotels.com/hkgnw Ideally located by Victoria Harbour, within easy reach of the shopping district,

Kowloon and Beyond at a Glance

places of interests, MTR and Star Ferry Pier. The hotel has 545 rooms and suites.

MID-RANGE / LOWER MID-RANGE / BOUTIQUE

Holiday Inn Golden Mile Hong Kong, 50 Nathan Road, Tsim Sha Tsui, Kowloon, tel: 852 2369 3111, www.holiday-inn.com/hongkong-gldn With a superb location in the heart of Tsim Sha Tsui in the Golden Mile area and with close proximity to MTR, Star Ferry Pier and Bus Terminus, and major attractions in the area, this hotel has 585 rooms and suites, with all the modern amenities.

The Luxe Manor, 39 Kimberley Road, Tsim Sha Tsui, Kowloon, tel: 852 3763 8888, www.theluxe manor.com Located in the heart of the Golden Mile, the Luxe Manor is a quirky design-driven boutique hotel with each room individually designed and styled in an eclectic mix of Oriental, post-modern and European decor with a touch of surrealism and fantasy, all boldly presented. The 159 rooms and suites have contemporary and hi-tech amenities.

The Salisbury YMCA of Hong Kong, 41 Salisbury Road, Tsim Sha Tsui, Kowloon, tel: 852 2736 0922, www.ymca-hotels.com/hongkong/ymcasalisbury A modest hotel in a prestigious location right across the harbour, near

the MTR, Star Ferry Pier and Harbour City shopping mall and steps away from harbour front attractions. It has 301 rooms and 62 suites, ideal for families, and the rooms are furnished with all the mod cons and broadband Internet access – special online rates are available.

The Kimberley Hotel, 28 Kimberley Road, Tsim Sha Tsui, Kowloon, tel: 852 2723 3888, www.kimberley hotels.com.hk Centrally located in the Golden Mile within easy reach of major attractions and the MTR, the Kimberley Hotel has 546 rooms and suites, all with modern amenities and facilities.

Eaton Hotel Hong Kong, 380 Nathan Road, Kowloon, tel: 852 2782 1818, http://hongkong.eatonhotels.com Located further up the Golden Mile on Nathan Road, this hotel is within easy reach of the major shopping areas and tourist attractions especially Temple Street and the Ladies' Market. It has 458 rooms and suites.

Metropark Hotel Mong Kok, 22 Lai Chi Kok Road, Mong Kok, Kowloon, tel: 852 2397 6683, www.metroparkhotelmongkok.com Sited in the heart of Mong Kok with its lively local ambience and several markets and tourist attractions in the area, and still within easy reach of the Golden Mile down the road, the Metropark has 430

rooms and suites – modestly furnished, yet functional and comfortable with all the modern amenities.

Dorsett Seaview Hotel, 268 Shanghai Street, Yau Ma Tei, Kowloon, tel: 852 2782 0882, www.dorsettseaview.com.hk Despite its name, it is not located by the harbour front, with reclamation getting in the way, but is located in the heart of Kowloon's very Chinese ethnic quarters. A great location to savour the local atmosphere with street markets and traditional shops, and it is also within a short distance of major attractions in the Golden Mile and Victoria Harbour. It has 268 rooms and suites, all comfortably furnished and equipped.

WHERE TO EAT

The numerous choices of cuisines and eateries in Kowloon reflect the nation's favourite pastime of eating and dining out. Whether it is feasting in upscale restaurants or dining in street cafés, the epicureans will be spoilt for choice. For a truly marvellous gastronomic experience, Hong Kong in general and Kowloon in particular are second to none. Miramar Shopping Centre, one of the largest shopping malls in Nathan Road, has no fewer than 18 restaurants and bars to choose from, while its neighbours, Knutsford Steps and Knutsford Terrace, are lively enclaves of entertainment and dining centres with many restaurants serving international cuisines.

Miramar Shopping Centre, 132–134 Nathan Road, Tsim Sha Tsui.

Knutsford Terrace/Knutsford Steps, 1 Kimberley Road, Tsim Sha Tsui (can be accessed via the shopping centre).

Harbour City mega-mall has 50 food and beverage outlets with both formal and informal dining. It is situated near Star Ferry Pier.

CHINESE CUISINE

Spring Moon, The Peninsula Hotel, Salisbury Road, Tsim Sha Tsui, Kowloon, tel: 852 2315 3160. This elegant restaurant, fitted out in nostalgic Art Deco period features, with stained glass and wood panelling reminiscent of an old Shanghai mansion, serves Cantonese and regional cuisine with signature dishes of roast pigeon marinated with cinnamon and roast Peking duck. A special feature is the tea counter which offers 25 selected Chinese teas, with professional tea masters in attendance to demonstrate the art of brewing and drinking tea. Opens 11:30–15:30 (lunch), 18:00–23:00 (dinner).

Loong Yuen Cantonese Restaurant, Basement 1, Holiday Inn Golden Mile, 50 Nathan Road, Tsim Sha Tsui, Kowloon, tel: 852 2315

1006. This award-winning restaurant is decked out with traditional paintings and artefacts as well as fish tanks with live fish for the menu. It features top quality dim sum and classic but innovative Cantonese fare, with award-winning shrimp fried rice, drunken shrimp flambé, braised Australian abalone with oyster sauce and Peking duck as examples of signature dishes. Opens 11:00–15:00 (lunch), 18:00–23:00 (dinner).

Celestial Court, 2/F, Sheraton Hong Kong Hotel & Towers, 20 Nathan Road, Tsim Sha Tsui, Kowloon, tel: 852 2369 1111 ext 3991. A spacious restaurant in traditional Chinese design with contemporary touches, serving fine Cantonese and regional dishes with award-winning dim sum dishes and roast suckling pig as one of the top signature dishes. Opens Mon–Sat 11:30–15:00 and Sun 10:30–15:00 (lunch), 18:00–23:30 (dinner).

Hutong, 28/F One Peking Building, Peking Road, Tsim Sha Tsui, Kowloon, tel: 852 3428 8342. One of the most popular restaurants in town, with stunning harbour views to match, it is a sophisticated outfit of classic chic, with antique furniture set in contemporary tones inspired by *hutongs* – Old Beijing courtyard homes. It serves innovative dishes based on northern Chinese cuisines, taking tradi-

tional recipes to a new dimension. The restaurant's signature dishes – such as bamboo clams in Chinese rose wine and chilli sauce, crispy deboned lamb ribs Hutong style and beggar chicken – are just a few examples of the gastronomic feast in store for you at this establishment. Opens 12:00–15:00 (lunch), 18:00 to midnight (dinner). Reservations are advisable, especially for window seats.

Yunyan Szechuan Restaurant, 4/F, Miramar Shopping Centre, 132 Nathan Road, Tsim Sha Tsui, Kowloon, tel: 852 2375 0800. Yunyan is a bright and spacious restaurant located in a big shopping mall. It features spicy and peppery Szechuan specialities prepared in authentic traditional style, with signature dishes of sautéed chicken with spicy red chillies and bean curd with minced meat and chillies among other regional goodies. Opens 11:30–15:00 (lunch), 17:30–23:30 (dinner).

STREET NOSH HONG KONG STYLE

Hing Kee Restaurant, 19 Temple Street, Yau Ma Tei, tel: 852 2384 3647. This is a simple restaurant but it is big when it comes to the flavours of Hong Kong favourites and is famed for its claypot rice and oyster omelette. Opens 17:30–01:00.

Tsui Wah Restaurant, G/F–1/F, 2 Carnarvon Road, Tsim Sha Tsui, Kowloon, tel: 852 2366 8250. A bustling fast-food atmosphere is prevalent at this restaurant, which serves all Hong Kong's local favourites. It is open for breakfast, lunch, dinner and supper with specialities such as home-made sliced fish balls and fish cakes with vermicelli in fish soup, sizzling king prawn with fried noodles Peking and Szechuan style, shredded pork and mushroom with fried noodles and Hainanese chicken rice among other local yummies. Opens 07:00–02:00.

Hang Heung's Kitchen, Shop L303, New World Centre, 18–24 Salisbury Road, Tsim Sha Tsui, Kowloon, tel: 852 2366 8628. This eating place features the favourite local staples, so it is a good place to go if you'd like to try dishes such as sampan *congee*, fish balls in rice noodles, wonton noodles and barbeque pork with rice, etc. Opens 07:00–23:00.

Mido Café, 63 Temple Street, Yau Ma Tei, Kowloon, tel: 852 2384 6402. This is a popular café with old-school decor. It serves all the local favourites, notably fluffy pineapple buns, oven-baked spare ribs, rice and fried noodles with sliced pork and other signature street dishes. Opens 08:30–21:30.

Lang Heung Noodles, 15A Austin Road, Tsim Sha Tsui, Kowloon, tel: 852 3173 8158. Serves an array of noodle dishes and local delicacies, with its signature dish of blanched beef tripe as a speciality. It is a popular place to go for both breakfast and lunch. It opens 08:00–03:00.

INTERNATIONAL AND WESTERN CUISINES

Felix, The Peninsula Hotel, Salisbury Road, Tsim Sha Tsui, Kowloon, tel: 852 2315 3188. Located on the 28th floor of The Peninsula tower, Felix is one of the swankiest restaurants in town, offering a grand dining experience 'on top of the world' with a commanding view of Victoria Harbour, Hong Kong Island and Kowloon, in a Philippe Starck-designed decor, featuring contemporary cuisine stylishly presented. The Wine Bar, American Bar and The Crazy Box, a mini discotheque, add to the excitement of the venue and make it a place to see and be seen. Opens 18:00–01:30 (drinks), 22:30–00:30 (snacks) and 18:00–22:00 (dinner).

Yamm, Ground Floor Lobby, The Mira Hong Kong, 118 Nathan Road, Tsim Sha Tsui, Kowloon, tel: 852 2315 5111. A chic restaurant with music and ambient lighting to create a stylish dining room serving international cuisine

in à la carte and semi-buffet style and featuring an array of Japanese delicacies and staples including sashimi, sushi, teppanyaki, yakatori and tempura as well as a selection of western dishes. Opens 11:30–14:30 (lunch) and 18:00–22:00 (dinner).

Nadaman, Lower Level 2, Kowloon Shangri-La, 64 Mody Road, Tsim Sha Tsui East, Kowloon, tel: 852 2721 2111. A calm minimalist atmosphere with a teppanyaki area and a traditional tatami room for those who want to dine in a traditional Japanese style. Nadaman serves the best of Japanese cuisine with signature dishes including teppanyaki Wagyu steak and *Kaiseki*, a traditional Japanese multi-course meal consisting of several small dishes. Opens 12:00–15:00 (lunch), 18:30–23:00 (dinner).

Aspasia, The Luxe Manor, 1st Floor, 39 Kimberley Road, Tsim Sha Tsui, Kowloon, tel: 852 3763 8800. An intimate Italian restaurant featuring modern Italian cuisine combined with a touch of influence from other national cuisines to create a contemporary menu including signatures dishes like veal chop with Jerusalem artichoke and Arabic coffee sauce, Japanese-style bouillabaisse with Italian lobster and Mediterranean prawns, and gourmet meat dishes of Grade 9 Wagyu beef, roast pigeon,

Kowloon and Beyond at a Glance

suckling pig, lamb rack and stuffed quail. Opens 12:00–14:30 (lunch), 15:00–18:00 (tea) and 18:30–23:00 (dinner).

Todai, Shop B1001–03, Miramar Shopping Centre, 132 Nathan Road, Tsim Sha Tsui, Kowloon, tel: 852 2375 9339. This is buffet heaven for big eaters! This large open-plan buffet restaurant serves a veritable cornucopia of Japanese and Asian dishes. The counters are laden with all kinds of food, the teppan lobster being the most popular; please note that diners are restricted to half a lobster per customer at a time. Opens 12:00–14:30 (lunch) and 18:30–22:30 (dinner).

Aqua, 29/30 Floors, One Peking Building, Peking Road, Tsim Sha Tsui, Kowloon, tel: 852 3427 2288. Another great venue for 'sky dining', this über-chic restaurant is perched on the penthouse floor of one of the swankiest buildings in Kowloon, with floor-to-ceiling windows to capture the breathtaking view of the harbour and glittering skyline. Adventurous and creative menus offering modern Italian cuisine are served in the Aqua Roma section, while the Aqua Tokyo showcases fine Japanese fares, and Aqua Spirit is a great place for a drink, where you can mingle with the in-crowd of the city. Opens Mon–Sat 12:00–15:30

(lunch), 12:00–16:00 (Sunday brunch), and 18:00–23:00 (dinner). Aqua Spirit is open 17:00–02:00.

Shopping in Kowloon takes retail therapy to new heights, with shops and shopping malls galore in every corner of Kowloon. The hub of the shopping district is Nathan Road, with wall-to-wall shops selling every imaginable product on the planet.

Miramar Shopping Centre, 132–134 Nathan Road, Tsim Sha Tsui, Kowloon. Located by Tsim Sha Tsui MTR station, this is the largest shopping mall in Nathan Road with 50,170m² (540,000 sq ft) of shopping space and six floors of retail outlets housing over 100 shops with lifestyle and trendy labels, including speciality shops, a cosmetic house and a fashion gallery.

Park Lane Shoppers Boulevard, 111–181 Nathan Road, Tsim Sha Tsui, Kowloon. Located opposite Miramar Shopping Centre and along Kowloon Park, Park Lane is a 300m-long (984ft) stretch of 50 shops with trendy fashion boutiques catering mainly to the young and young at heart. It is a pleasant place to shop, away from the crowded shopping precincts on the opposite side of Nathan Road.

Harbour City, 5 Canton Road, Tsim Sha Tsui,

Kowloon (take the MTR to Tsim Sha Tsui and go through the Ocean Terminal entrance near Star Ferry Pier). This is the biggest one-stop shopping and entertainment complex in Hong Kong, with 185,800m² (2 million square feet) of retail space featuring over 700 shops (mostly of branded designer labels), 50 food and beverage outlets, three hotels and two cinemas.

Elements, 1 Austin Road West, West Kowloon (Kowloon is the nearest MTR station). The latest addition to the shopping galaxy of Hong Kong, this design-driven mega-mall of 92,900m² (1 million square feet) is themed after the five elements of Chinese philosophy, with each element representing one of the themes of the mall – fire for entertainment, metal for luxury goods, water for food and beverage, earth represents fashion, and wood is for the health and beauty section. It is a lifestyle destination with 123 shops, an ice rink and entertainment centre including a 1600-seat grand cinema.

Chinese Arts and Crafts, Star House, 3 Salisbury Road, Tsim Sha Tsui (nearest MTR), Kowloon (there are also branches in Central and Wan Chai). This is a great place to find high-quality Chinese products including paintings, jade and semiprecious stone carvings and statues, silk soft furnishings and jewellery. A wide choice of handicrafts can be found here.

Yue Hwa Chinese Emporium, 301–309, Nathan Road, Tsim Sha Tsui (nearest MTR), Kowloon (there are branches in Peking Road and Central). A large emporium dedicated to all things Chinese, from furniture and paintings to embroidery, traditional jackets and clothes for men and women, jewellery, sculptures, etc.

TOURS AND EXCURSIONS

A convenient way to take in the sights of Kowloon and New Territories is to join local tours provided by licensed tour companies.

Hong Kong Tourism Board (HKTB) has some interesting 'Meet the People' programmes whereby visitors can experience the living culture of Hong Kong. Visitors can join free classes on Chinese culture, from traditional practices such as feng shui, t'ai chi and kung fu to antiques and jewellery appreciation, Chinese tea appreciation and Chinese cake-making. One can even learn the secrets of Chinese traditional medicine. There are also architecture walks (at a fee of HK$100) in Central District with members of the Hong Kong Institute of Architects. Programmes are subject to change. For details and reservation of the above classes, contact HKTB Visitor

Hotline on tel: 852 2508 1234. Brochures with details can be obtained from any HKTB offices (the main one in Kowloon is at Star Ferry Concourse).

Travel Asia (HK) Ltd, 17/F, 10 Knutsford Terrace, Tsim Sha Tsui, Kowloon, tel: 852 2721 0222, www.travelasia.com.hk **Target Travel & Tours Services**, 9/F, Chinachem Cameron Centre, 42 Cameron Road, Tsim Sha Tsui, Kowloon, tel: 852 2312 1812, targett@netvigator.com

Duk Ling: A delightful way to cruise the harbour is in this last remaining traditional Chinese junk with its famous red sails, with a one-hour cruise of Victoria Harbour departing from Kowloon Public Pier by Star Ferry Pier 14:00 and 16:00 (Thu), 10:00 and 12:00 (Sat). It is also available for private charters. For reservations, contact HKTB Visitor Hotline, tel: 852 2508 1234. The cost of the fare is HK$50. **Note:** Visitors are required to show their passport and register in advance in person at the HKTB Visitors Centre at Star Ferry Concourse.

The Big Bus Company Kowloon By Night: Enjoy a panoramic night tour of Kowloon from an open-top bus on a one-hour jaunt with recorded running commentary in a choice of eight

languages to see the bright lights of the city. Depart from Avenue of Stars next to Starbucks at 19:00 before the Symphony of Lights, and at 20:30 after the show. For details, tel: 852 2723 2108, www.bigbustours.com (day tours available).

DIY Cruise: If you want the freedom of an independent sea adventure, you can charter your own boat and sail around the waters in Hong Kong, picnicking at secluded coves or visiting some of the outlying islands. **Viking's Charters and Co. Ltd.** offers a de luxe yacht, motorized cruiser and Chinese pleasure junk for the day or evening. The boats are spacious, well equipped and have showers. Sample price starts from HK$2800 per boat for an eight-hour day cruise on a Chinese pleasure junk with a capacity of 30 passengers, and HK$2500 for a five-hour evening charter. Prices include a crew of two or three, depending on the size of the boats. The pick-up points are at Central Pier/Causeway Bay Public Pier/Kowloon Public Pier. Boats can sail anywhere that allows anchorage in Hong Kong. For details, contact Viking's Charters and Co. Ltd., tel: 852 2814 9899 or 852 2576 8992, info@vikingscharters.com.hk www.boatandboating.com

5
New Territories

The New Territories encompasses the large expanse of territory between Kowloon and the Chinese border, as well as the outlying islands. This area was leased to the British for 99 years from the Qing Dynasty in 1898 after the signing of the Second Convention of Peking to extend the Hong Kong territory. In 1997, it was handed over to the People's Republic of China along with Hong Kong Island and the Kowloon Peninsula. It covers an area of 952km² (367 sq miles) with over 3.57 million people and a population density of 3748 per square kilometre.

The New Territories are defined mostly by forested mountains and valleys, dramatic coastline and townships redolent of Hong Kong before its modern urban development. The designated urban areas were created to accommodate the overspill from Kowloon and Hong Kong Island, with satellite towns known as 'new towns' being built with inexpensive high-rise flats to accommodate the increasing population. Shopping centres and schools are set up to make the towns self-sufficient and railways constructed to provide convenient commuting for the residents who work in downtown Hong Kong. The new towns are well planned, and 2.26 million trees and shrubs were planted in 2006 to create parks and gardens as recreational areas and serve as green lungs for the estates. However, most of the land in the New Territories is rural and reserved for parklands and nature reserves. If you have a day to spare, it is worth a day trip to get away from the shadows of the

Opposite: *The pagoda of the Ten Thousand Buddhas Monastery.*

skyscrapers in downtown Hong Kong to a completely different aspect of Hong Kong. Within an hour's journey from Kowloon, the landscape is more rural with scenic mountainous terrain clad in greenery and forest, ideal for hiking. Downtown Hong Kong seems like a different planet among this wild beauty. There are no quaint villages any more but there are still remnants of traditional houses, clan houses and temples. The nature reserves and wetlands are of ecological interest and illustrate the Hong Kong government's effort to provide a green belt in the country.

EASTERN NEW TERRITORIES
Lion Rock Country Park ★

This country park covers an area of 5.7km² (2.2 sq miles) at an elevation of 495m (1624ft) above sea level. The park is named after a **natural rock formation** shaped like a sitting lion and can only be accessed via a winding footpath leading to the top of the head of the 'lion', affording a panoramic view of the city and Hong Kong Island in the distance. It is popular with hikers,

picnickers and nature lovers. Nearby is another strange rock formation called the **Amah Rock** (or Mong Fu Shek in Chinese), in the shape of a woman carrying a child. Legend has it that a fisherman's wife would stand at this spot with her child every day, waiting for her husband to return from the sea and not knowing that he had drowned. Tin Hau, the Goddess of the Sea, felt sorry for them and turned them into stone so that their spirits could join her husband. It has become a symbol of loyalty and faithfulness for Chinese women who would come here to worship the stone.

This is another vantage point from which to see the Sha Tin District. The forested hills here are home to black-eared kites – migratory birds from Asia and Australia. Long-tail macaques are also found here in abundance, and can cause mischief by begging for food from visitors. It is advisable not to feed them as they can be aggressive and unpredictable. These monkeys are not indigenous to these hills but were descended from monkeys released here in the 1920s.

Sha Tin *

Across the border from Kowloon lies Sha Tin District, covering an area of about 70km² (27 sq miles) in eastern New Territories. Once a rural market town, Sha Tin is now part of the New Town development, with a well-developed infrastructure and peppered with high-rise flats. It is considered to be a great example of a well-planned new town and is often showcased by the government to visiting foreign dignitaries. There are a few tourist attractions in the area. For a start, it is home to the second racecourse in Hong Kong. **Sha Tin Racecourse** is a world-class race track and was built in 1978 on reclaimed land. It is larger than Happy Valley Racecourse (*see* panel, page 35) and has a capacity for 85,000 people, with two grandstands and 23 stables with room for 1260 horses. The racecourse has an equine hospital and an equine swimming pool to exercise the horses, and also the world's longest 'Diamond Vision' television screen. Major races include Cathay Pacific International Races;

LOK MA CHAU

This village at the border with mainland China is on the itinerary of tours to the New Territories. The border crossing point between Hong Kong and mainland China lies just south of the Shenzhen River (or Sham Chun River in Cantonese) and is known as the Frontier Closed Area (FCA). First established in 1951 and expanded in 1962 by the Hong Kong government, this buffer zone covers an area of 28km² (11 sq miles) to prevent illegal immigrants sneaking into Hong Kong from China. For local residents this area is restricted to Closed Area permit holders only. The buffer zone with fences and immigration control points is pristine without any human habitation and has become a natural wildlife sanctuary. There is a proposal to reduce the buffer zone to 8km² (3 sq miles) by 2010 but wildlife conservationists are concerned it will have a negative ecological effect. Tour companies take tourists to a vantage point on a hill to observe the buffer zone overlooking the fenced wildlife reserve with the busy city of Shenzhen just beyond the fence. The hill is a local beauty spot with a pavilion and a telescope to take a close-up view of Shenzhen. It is quite interesting to be in Hong Kong and look into mainland China separated just by a fence.

Queen Elizabeth II Cup; Asian Champion Mile and Mercedes Hong Kong Derby among others. The racecourse offers a 'Tourist Experience' on race day, which includes the 'Racing In Style' package with an all-round racing experience complete with racing tips, and a 'Come Horseracing Tour' offering the excitement of day and night races including special dining and admission privileges with access to the Members' Enclosure. The Tourist Badge will gain free access to Members' Betting Halls and trackside areas. Sha Tin Racecourse can be reached by the Racecourse MTR on the East Rail Line.

Ten Thousand Buddhas Monastery **

This unique temple is famous for its plethora of Buddha statues, with many more Buddhas than its name suggests. It is situated on the hills overlooking Pai Tau Village in Sha Tin and is only suitable for people who are fit and have the stamina to climb over 400 steps up the hill to reach the monastery. If you can scale the hill, you will be rewarded with a spectacular sight – thousands of Buddhas and Lohans (Buddha's disciples). Golden statues of Lohans in various forms and postures line the way up to the temple. At the forecourt, more Buddha statues stand guard along the wall.

It was founded by the **Reverend Yuet Kai** in 1949 and completed in 1957. It covers 8ha (20 acres) over two levels. The lower temple complex consists of the main temple; a nine-storey pagoda; pavilions with principle Buddhist deities including Kwan Yin, the Goddess of Mercy, flanked by the 18 Arhans, Buddha's chosen apostles – nine on the west and nine on the east of the monastery. The main temple houses 12,800 miniature Buddha statues spectacularly lined up on the wall, each statue in a different *mudra* or prayer gesture. At the central altar, encased in a glass case, is the embalmed body of Reverend Yuet Kai clad in a red and gold monk's robe and covered in gold leaf. The red pagoda is a famous landmark in Hong Kong and has appeared on a HK$100 bill. Each storey contains Buddhas in different *mudra*. By the main temple is a vegetarian restaurant with a capacity for 100 people at a time. The upper level is designated to the Temple of the God of Heaven; Temple of the Candi Buddha, the mother of Buddha; Temple of Amita Buddha and Kwan Tei, the God of Righteousness, riding on a horse – he has become the patron saint of horse racing and jockeys and gamblers often pray to him for winnings. The Kwan Yin Temple here used to face the sea to protect fishermen but now, with reclamation, the sea view is obscured. To get there, go to Sha Tin on the East Rail Line, station Exit B, and via a ramp to Pai Tau Village, past white Po Fook Hill Temple, up a narrow path and follow the sign to the temple up the hill.

Hong Kong Heritage Museum *

To preserve the cultural heritage of Hong Kong, this museum has 12 galleries of exhibitions covering history, art and culture, with 20,000 exhibits from the New Territories and neighbouring regions. There are Cantonese opera relics, including costumes, props, scripts and musical instruments; documentary materials and photographs; folk art; toys, comics and designs to reflect contemporary living in the 21st century; modern art; and Chinese paintings and calligraphy. There is also a great collection of Chinese antiquities showcasing Chinese ceramics, clay sculptures, stone carving, jade ware, lacquer ware, furniture and Tibetan artefacts and religious paintings. The museum is located at 1 Man Lam Road (by the Shing Mun River), Sha Tin. It is open Mon and Wed–Sat 10:00–18:00, Sun and public holidays 10:00–19:00. It is closed on Tue (except public holidays) and the first two days of Chinese New Year. To get there, travel to Che Kung Temple Station on the KCR line followed by a five-minute walk, or Sha Tin Station on East Rail Line with a 15-minute walk.

Above: *One of the many thousands of Buddhas in the Ten Thousand Buddhas Monastery. Each storey of the pagoda is dedicated to Buddha in a different mudra.*

Sai Kung Town, once a sleepy fishing enclave, is now a built-up area of residential and commercial buildings. The **Sai Kung Promenade** is renowned for its seafood restaurants and has been aptly called 'Seafood Street'. There are shops, boutiques and many Western and Asian eateries along the seafront. Explore the local markets, temples and streets to soak up the ethnic culture and colours. To get there, from Hang Hau MTR Exit B1 take green minibus 101M, or from Choi Hung MTR Exit C2 take green minibus 1A to Sai Kung Town Terminus. There are several buses from Sai Kung Market to Sai Kung East Country Park.

SAI KUNG PENINSULA ★★

Dubbed as the 'Back Garden' of Hong Kong, much of the Sai Kung Peninsula is protected as parkland to create a recreational area in a rural and coastal setting. **The Sai Kung East Country Park** is like a soothing balm to the city dwellers who come here for a breath of fresh air amid their hectic urban lifestyle. Sai Kung East Country Park is surrounded by scenic spots dominated by **Sharp Peak**, a conical mountain towering 468m (1536ft) above the lowlands and popular with experienced hikers. The view over Tai Long Wan Bay with its four famous **beaches** – Sai Wan, Ham Tin, Tai Long and Tung Wan – is stunning.

Lam Tsuen Wishing Tree ★

Another favourite stop for tourists is this old camphor tree, dubbed the 'Wishing Tree', at Lam Tsuen in Tai Po. The original village was established about 700 years ago in the Sung Dynasty. Today Lam Tsuen District spreads over 26 villages in the area. The local people believe the tree, which the Lam Tsuen Valley Committee claimed is a camphor tree and not a banyan tree as was widely thought, has spiritual power and can grant wishes. A stone tablet dedicated to Pak Kung, the Earth God and Protector of Villagers, is enshrined under the tree. Legend has it that a worshipper had a son with learning difficulties but after praying for his son at the tree, the boy made remarkable academic progress. Word began to spread of the magical power of the tree and people began to flock there to make wishes. They would write their wishes on red papers and hang them on the tree and soon the whole tree was heavily weighed down with the red paper wishes. The tree began to wither, shed its leaves and hollow out. The local authority decided to save the tree by banning worshippers from hanging any prayer papers – they fenced the tree in and propped up the damaged branches with wooden poles. Instead, wooden racks on which to hang the paper prayers were built by the tree. A small stall by the tree sells scrolls of paper prayers with calligraphy and religious drawings, and for HK$5 you can buy a scroll on which to write your wishes and tie it to the rack with red plastic string.

Nearby is a temple built in the Qing Dynasty and dedicated to Tin Hau, the Goddess of the Sea. During religious festivals, people from as far as Aberdeen, Lei Yue Mun and Sai Kung – all coastal settlements – come here to worship and make offerings to Tin Hau and the various deities in the temple.

WESTERN NEW TERRITORIES

This region is rich in heritage, with old temples, ancient pagodas and a walled village, and is also renowned for its wetlands and nature reserves.

Ching Chung Koon **

Among the crowded high-rise residential buildings in Tuen Mun District in western New Territories lies an oasis of spiritual tranquillity in the Ching Chung Koon temple complex. Its name means 'Evergreen Pine Temple' and it is a picture of serenity with its cluster of pavilions, pagodas, ornamental archways and towers, all ornately designed and painted in bright, garish colours. The red pillars are particularly eye-catching. The main triple gateway is a work of art – Chinese religious motifs in an intricate riot of red, white, green, blue and gold hues. The main building, called the Palace of Pure Brightness, is enshrined with various deities. The big ancestral hall houses the ashes of deceased devotees which are kept among hundreds of lighted lamps. At the bottom of the compound lies a lovely Chinese garden complete with pavilions, water features, fish ponds and a bronze statue of the founder. It

Below: *The traditional triple gateway of the Ching Chung Koon temple complex is a marvellous work of art, with its intricately painted Chinese religious motifs in a spectrum of auspicious colours.*

PUI PUI THE CROC

Pui Pui, a saltwater crocodile, is the star of the **Hong Kong Wetland Park**. It was found on 2 November 2003 in the Shan Pui River in northwest New Territories when it was just a juvenile. Its mysterious appearance in the river led to the speculation that it could have been an illegal pet that managed to escape from its owner, or it may have been dumped there when it grew too big to handle. Whatever its past is, it has found a sanctuary at the wetland park, living a pampered life in a $72m^2$ (775-sq-ft) enclosure fenced up with a high acrylic wall to enable the public to view it without causing distress. The simulation of its natural habitat has infrared heaters and heat pads to keep it warm and a pond to serve as its own private swimming pool. When it was first found, a territory-wide competition was held to find a name for it. Over 1000 entries were received and the authority picked the name 'Pui', which means the 'Precious One', and also because it was found in the Shan Pui River. Since then it has been affectionately known as Pui Pui. Like most superstars it has grown used to the admiring crowd. The fact that Pui Pui was found abandoned has aroused public concern and awareness of wildlife conservation in the wetlands.

was originally built as a rural retreat in 1949. A clinic of traditional Chinese medicine offers subsidized medical services to the local residents. Huge bronze incense urns are installed in front of the various prayer halls. The temple is famous for its bonsai show, which takes place in April or May every year. To get there, go to Siu Hong MTR Exit B, then change to Light Rail 505 and alight at Ching Chung Station with a five-minute walk.

Hong Kong Wetland Park **

The wetland park covers more than 60ha (148 acres), with well-planned boardwalks and walking trails along the marshland from which to observe the wildlife. It is an idyllic setting – the shimmering waters of the marshland interspersed with water lilies and aquatic plants as wooden walkways criss-cross the marshes – with mountain ranges looming in the distance in mainland China across the border. The tranquillity is, however, just a short distance from the many high-rise residential buildings across the road. Nevertheless, you can shut out all the bustle of the town as you stroll through the beautiful wetland park to catch glimpses of egrets, storks, ducks, herons and other waterfowl. Colourful butterflies flutter among the aquatic plants and dragonflies perch high on the water grass, out of reach of the frogs. Ripples in the water betray the presence of the fish waiting for a chance to pounce on the insects skirting over the water.

The wetland park is situated on the northern tip of Tin Shui Wan in the Yuen Long District near the Chinese border. It was set up to conserve the marshland, to protect the ecosystem of the diverse wildlife in this habitat, not to mention to protect it from property developers. Its mission is 'to foster awareness, knowledge and understanding of the inherent value of the wetlands through the East Asian region and beyond' by creating an educational and recreational wetland park to muster public support for wetland conservation. The **Visitors' Centre** should be the first port of call before embarking on to the boardwalks. This centre provides valuable information on the wetlands, with Wetland Interactive World (featuring themed exhibition galleries), a theatre and an indoor play area with 'Swamp Adventure' to amuse younger visitors. The resource centre provides a host of information on the importance of wetlands and its biodiversity.

The main attraction of the centre is a saltwater crocodile named **Pui Pui** (*see* panel, page 80) kept in a special enclosure built to simulate its natural habitat. The park recreated habitats specially designed for waterfowl and other wildlife, with wooden walkways featuring Stream Walk, Succession Walk and Mangrove Boardwalk. There are three bird hides, built near the mudflats, fish pond and riverside, to enable visitors to observe birds in their natural habitats. To get there, go to Tin Shui Wan MTR station Exit E1, then change for Light Rail route 705, 706 or 761 and alight at the Wetland Park stop, with a five-minute walk. Alternatively, take bus 967 from Admiralty (West) Bus Terminus at Drake Street outside Lippo Centre and get off at Grandeur Terrace bus stop, then a three-minute walk to the entrance. Allow at least half day to enjoy the wetland. It is open Mon, Wed–Sun and public holidays 10:00–17:00, closed Tue (except public holidays).

MANGROVE BOARDWALK

The Mangrove Boardwalk at Hong Kong Wetland Park is a fascinating experience; you get up close to the denizens of the mangrove habitat, particularly the fiddler crabs, with each male crab waving its oversized single claw to attract the females. Mudskippers slither about on the mud with gills flared and flapping as the males show aggression to other males to protect their territory. These strange-looking fish are amphibious and so can live on the muddy banks without being in the water.

Below: *A tranquil scene in Hong Kong Wetland Park – a great escape from the shadows of the city skyscrapers.*

Above: *Tai Fu Tai, an elegant 19th-century Mandarin's mansion built by the Man clan, is a fine example of the grand lifestyle of the scholar-gentry class in the Qing Dynasty.*

Tai Fu Tai ★★★

Step back in time to the grandeur of a 19th-century Mandarin's mansion when you go through the gate of Tai Fu Tai (Noble Man's Mansion). It is situated at Wing Ping Tsuen of San Tin north of Yuen Long District. It is one of the most elegant buildings in the territory and is a fine example of the residence of the scholar-gentry class in the Qing Dynasty (1644–1911). It was built in 1865 by **Man Chung-luen** of the Man clan, whose roots were originally in Sichuan but the clan later migrated to Jiangxi and Guangdong during the Song Dynasty (960–1279). The Man clan is one of the Five Great Clans in Hong Kong, with a track record of scholastic prominence and imperially linked family. One of their ancestors, Man Tin-cheung, was a famous patriot at the end of the dynasty. The Mans had settled in the San Tin area since the 15th century. Man Chung-luen was a member of the 21st generation of the Man clan. He was a scholar who had passed the highest imperial examination (*see* panel, page 83) and became a very successful merchant. He was a renowned philanthropist and the Qing emperor recognized his generosity by bestowing the title 'Tai Fu' or 'Noble Man' in recognition of his good work.

Tai Fu Tai is an elaborately designed house built in a traditional Chinese architectural style: shaped like a mini fortress with very solid granite base and green brick works. The large compound is surrounded by stone walls. Like all Chinese mansions of prominent families, it has a **grand entrance** with the name of 'Tai Fu Tai' etched in gold on a red wooden board flanked by two smaller side entrances, possibly for less important visitors or staff. The entrance opens into a second gateway which leads to an open **courtyard** leading in turn to the main hall with side chambers and bedrooms. The entrance to the **main hall** is framed by an ornate blue wooden frame with Chinese motifs. Under the eaves of the main hall are two **honorific boards** bestowed on the parents and grandparents of Man Chung-luen by the Qing Emperor Guangxu in 1875, engraved in Chinese and Manchu characters, believed to be the only examples of their kind in Hong Kong. Between the two honorific boards is a wooden **title tablet** given by Wen Zhou-xun, a Qing official, to honour the master of the house as was common practice in Imperial China. In the main hall are **portraits** of Man Chung-luen, his wife and other members of his family dressed in very grand traditional costumes of that era. On the left of the main hall are the scholar's study and an enclosed courtyard with a Western design influence, while the right section opens into a corridor through a moon-gate to the kitchen, servants' quarters and the lavatory. The primitive **kitchen** has several wood-burning stoves and three massive woks to cater for the big household. Two sets of stone millstones lie on the floor, which would have been used to grind grain for the family.

When touring round the house it is worth noting the many beautiful plaster mouldings, wood carvings and murals of auspicious Chinese motifs such as plum blossoms, chrysanthemums, orchids, bamboo and animals like deer, bats, unicorns and dragons along the eaves, doorways and walls and even on the roof and façade of the house. Western influence can be seen in some of the plaster mouldings featuring Baroque floral design

IMPERIAL EXAMINATION

The historical importance of education in Chinese culture is attributed mainly to the teachings of Confucius, who reputedly proclaimed: 'Those who work with their heads will rule, while those who work with their hands will serve.' Another saying on the importance of education was that 'books will hold a thousand measures of grain and in books are found houses of gold'. The Imperial Examination or *Keju* was first set up during the Sui Dynasty (581–618) and continued until the Qing Dynasty (1644–1911) to give people from all social classes, except slaves and women, an equal opportunity to sit for examinations. Examinations were held at various levels starting with local (entrance), progressing to district, provincial and finally the palace examination under supervision of the emperor. It was based on memorizing the Confucius classic namely *The Four Books and The Five Classics*; composing an eight-part essay called the 'Eight-Legged Essay'; being skilled in civil law; analyzing political problems; calligraphy; poetry and art. Examinations lasted from 24 to 72 hours and took place in sparse cells. Very few people attained the highest level of the Imperial Examination, known as *Jinshi*. Those who did were rewarded with high-ranking jobs in the civil service or even ministerial posts and would bring honour to their families.

TSING MA BRIDGE

This spectacular bridge holds the record for the longest road-rail suspension bridge in the world, spanning the Ma Wan Channel for 2.2km (1.4 miles), with the main span stretching for 1377m (1506yd). It links the New Territories and Lantau Island with Hong Kong International Airport on Chek Lap Kok. The suspension bridge was named after the first words of the two islands, Tsing Yi and Ma Wan, that straddle the gap between the New Territories and Lantau Island. It was officially opened by the British Prime Minister Margaret Thatcher on 27 April 1997, just before the handover. The double-decker bridge has two rail tracks on the lower deck, complemented by two lanes for motor vehicles in case of emergency, while the upper deck has a six-lane motorway. The total length of wire to hold up the suspension is 160,000km (100,000 miles), reputedly long enough to go four times round the world. It was built by an Anglo-Japanese construction joint venture at a cost of HK$7.14 billion. It has become one of the famous landmarks in Hong Kong and at night the whole bridge is aglow with lights. Lantau Link Visitor Centre & Viewing Platform on the northwest corner of Tsing Yi Island has more information on the bridge. The centre opens 10:00–17:00 weekdays (closed Wed), 10:00–18:30 Sat, Sun and public holidays.

along with the painted glass panes. The large compound has an ornate Chinese garden on the right with stone garden furniture and potted plants in stone pots. There are a few lodges at the front of the house (but within its compound), probably to house the staff. One can imagine the grand lifestyle of the Man clan in the mansion. It was occupied by them until the 1980s and it was declared a national monument in July 1987. It is open daily (including public holidays) 09:00–13:00 and 14:00–17:00 (closed Tue and the first three days of Chinese New Year, Christmas Day and Boxing Day). Admission is free. To get there, from Sheung Shui KCR station, take bus 76K (opposite station) and alight at San Tin near the post office. Then follow signs to Tai Fu Tai and walk for 5–10 minutes along Castle Peak Road (the mansion is surrounded by modern buildings and flats).

Man Lun Fung Ancestral Hall ★★

Round the corner from Tai Fu Tai is another great monument of the Man clan, located in Fan Tin Tsuen in San Tin where the clan built at least five ancestral halls to revere and worship their ancestors. This particular ancestral hall was built in honour of Man Lun-fun, a member of the eighth generation of the Man clan, around the end of the 17th century. Built in traditional style, it features three halls with two enclosed courtyards in between. The entrance hall is named 'To Shu Tong', literally meaning the 'hall of scholars'. It is a beautiful building with many wonderful period features such as grand stone columns and ornate carvings on the eaves, doorways and roof. Opening times are the same as for Tai Fu Tai.

Kam Tin Walled City (Kat Hing Wai) ★★

Situated east of Yuen Long, this is the most renowned walled village in the New Territories. It was built during the Ming Dynasty in the 1600s by the Tang clan, one of the Five Great Clans who settled in the New Territories. It is a rectangular walled village with an area of 100x90m (328x295ft), its narrow terraced houses cramped within the wall. Small alleyways run between shabby houses which are mostly modernized. Four hundred descendants of the Tang clan still live here, mostly elderly people. The women still wear traditional costumes with wide-brimmed hats covered in black cloth with fringes round the brim. Visitors who wish to take their pictures would be asked to pay HK$10 for the privilege.

Walled villages were built for protection against pirates, bandits and wild tigers. During the Qing Dynasty, the village was surrounded by a 5m-high (16ft) wall of blue bricks with cannon towers, protected by a moat. Today the village is protected by a 5.5m-thick (18ft) wall with remnants of the moat. It was the last village to fall under the control of the British in the 1800s. During one of the skirmishes in 1899, the villagers barricaded themselves within the walled village but the British proved too strong for them. The British blasted the iron gates open, removed them and shipped them back to Britain as the spoils of war. In 1924, a member of the Tang clan petitioned the British government to return the gates. As a gesture of goodwill, the gates were returned on 26 May 1925 by the 16th Governor, Sir Reginald Stubbs, when he personally went to Kam Tin for a ceremonial return of the gates. Today, there is a tablet hanging near the gate citing the incident.

Below: *Kam Tin Walled City still maintains its original walls and residents adhere to old traditions, but the houses inside have been modernized and updated.*

Kam Tin Walled City is the private property of the Tang clan and it has not yet been declared a national monument. Admission fee is a donation of HK$1 per person. As it is not easy to get there by public transport, it is better to join a tour of the New Territories that will include a visit there. Otherwise take the West Rail Line to Kam Sheung Road Station and ask for directions to get there.

6
Lantau Island

The South China Sea within the territory of Hong Kong is peppered with 260 outlying islands. The two largest islands – Lantau and Lamma – are the most popular with tourists. There are a number of interesting attractions and sights that offer a great day trip or overnighter from the bustle of the metropolis in Hong Kong Island and Kowloon. Efficient transport facilities offer easy access to the islands and there is a choice of accommodation for an overnight stay.

Lantau Island is the largest island in Hong Kong, spanning a total area of 146km² (56 sq miles), twice the size of Hong Kong Island. It is endowed with wild beauty – picturesque forest-clad mountains and a scenic coastline. The highest peak on the island is in the Phoenix mountain range, rising to a summit of 935m (3068ft), making it the second highest peak in Hong Kong (after Tai Mo Shan in the New Territories) and twice as high as Victoria Peak. The rugged terrain is largely untouched by development, with 78.4km² (30 sq miles) of wild country park ideal for country pursuits. It serves as the green lung of the country, with relatively few high-rise developments compared with Kowloon and Hong Kong Island. It has a population of 45,000 spread over 47 villages dotted around the island of which **Mui Wo**, **Tai O** and **Tung Chung** are being developed into new towns with high-rise residential and commercial buildings. **Discovery Bay** on the north-eastern coast is a private development with an up-market community complete with a golf club,

Opposite: *Tian Tan Giant Buddha stands guard over Ngong Ping Village.*

THE MAGIC OF WALT DISNEY

Walt Elias Disney, born in Chicago on 5 December 1901, is hailed as one of the world's greatest motion picture producers and harbinger of family entertainment of its kind. He was a visionary who had an instinct that animals would appeal more than humans in cartoon films of that era. He was contracted to Universal Studios® to create an animated series featuring a rabbit called 'Oswald the Lucky Rabbit' but when his contract was not renewed he struck out on his own to do animated films, initially without much success. While working for the Pesman Art Studio in Kansas City in 1919, he met Ub Iwerks, a cartoonist and animator, and they forged a strong partnership working on various animal characters, but none really inspired Disney until Iwerks created a character supposedly based on a pet mouse that Disney used to own. Originally Disney wanted to call it Mortimer Mouse but his wife Lillian persuaded him to call it Mickey Mouse. It was to become the most iconic mouse in the world. Later Minnie Mouse was created to be his companion.

marine club and their own man-made beach. But in recent years Lantau Island has been brought to the forefront of development (the country parks remained as conservation areas) with the opening of **Hong Kong International Airport**, **Hong Kong Disneyland®** and **Ngong Ping 360 Village**. Visitors to the island have increased and the population will rise when the new towns are developed. The once sleepy fishing villages are slowly awakening to modern development, hopefully with their natural beauty intact.

HONG KONG DISNEYLAND® RESORT ★★★

Disneyland® has travelled east once again and opened its second theme park in Asia after Tokyo Disney Resort® in Japan. It was officially opened on 12 September 2005. Developed as a joint venture of the Walt Disney Company® and the government of Hong Kong, this is Disney's first undertaking in China with the aim to attract visitors from mainland China and other Asian countries. It is a world-class development covering an area of 125.5ha (310 acres) on reclaimed land at Penny's Bay on the northeastern corner of Lantau Island. In true Disney style, Hong Kong Disneyland® Resort is a fantastically designed theme park that blends Disney's wondrous fairytales and themes using modern technology with special sensitivity to the local culture. Feng shui masters were consulted on the designs of the park and resorts, and one of the main hotel ballrooms has a dimension of 888m² (9558 sq ft) in accordance to the Chinese auspicious numbering system – the word for 'eight' sounds similar to the word for 'prosperity' in Cantonese. The hotel lifts do not have 'No. 4' level as 'four' sounds like 'death' in Cantonese. Announcements and signage are in English, Mandarin and Cantonese. The Disney kingdom comprises Hong Kong Disneyland® Park and two themed hotels – the Hong Kong Disneyland® Hotel and Disney's Hollywood Hotel and Inspiration Lake Recreation Centre. The areas outside Disneyland® theme park are beautifully landscaped with flower gardens, sweeping lawns, palm trees and the lakeside park.

Hong Kong Disneyland® Park

The theme park offers a full day of timeless entertainment and fun in a make-believe world of fantasy, magical experience and adventure with Disney classic attractions and Broadway-like live entertainment. True to its mantra of 'leave today

and enter the world of yesterday, tomorrow and fantasy', it provides a thrilling experience and fun for families and people of all ages. It's a full-on show all day with very friendly and efficient service – staff members are known as 'the cast' and visitors are referred to as 'guests'. Junior visitors are thrilled by the appearances of much-loved Disney characters starring Mickey Mouse and Minnie Mouse along with a stellar cast such as Donald Duck, Goofy, Cinderella, Stitch, Winnie the Pooh, Alice in Wonderland and Snow White among others. Entertainers, jugglers, clowns, musicians and other Disney characters provide street entertainment all day throughout the park, especially around Main Street USA®. The park is designed by **Walt Disney Imagineering**, the innovative organization that creates all the Disney theme parks, attractions and resort hotels, and is compacted into showcasing only the finest elements from other Disney destinations. It is the smallest Disneyland® in the world but its attractions capture the essence of the magic kingdom with the added advantage that it can be covered in one day, saving time and cost if visitors have a tight schedule and do not have the time to do a two-day visit like in the other bigger Disneyland® resorts.

There are four themed attractions: **Main Street USA®**, **Fantasyland**, **Tomorrowland®** and **Adventureland**. The Park Promenade leading to Disneyland® Park is filled with an air of anticipation of a magical time ahead,

Above: *Mickey Mouse welcomes visitors with open arms at the Hong Kong Disneyland® Resort, a great family entertainment theme park with wonderful thrills and adventures for all who pass through the gate to the magical world of Disney.*

with a carnival atmosphere. Mickey Mouse stands atop the gate, welcoming visitors to his kingdom with open arms. A large fountain with Mickey Mouse, Minnie Mouse, Goofy and other Disney characters surfing on the fountain foams adds to the excitement, especially for the children. After the toll gate is a large flower bed landscaped with the face of Mickey Mouse smiling at visitors from an embankment in front of the Disney train station. The main entrance leads to Main Street USA®.

Main Street USA®

Modelled after small-town America of the 1890–1910 era, it is redolent of the vibrant boulevards and civic plazas of Walt Disney's youth. This is the main thoroughfare of the park, abounding with gift shops selling Disney merchandise, eateries and entertainment arcades. Old-fashioned steam trains of the **Hong Kong Disneyland® Railroad** embark from the train station here to take a grand circle tour of the theme park, calling at Fantasyland Station. The daily **Disney Parade** throngs through here and tends to be packed with visitors during show time. **High School Musical** is performed live every day at the bottom of the street, usually drawing a large crowd. At the end of Main Street, the fairytale Sleeping Beauty Castle, **Aurora**, looms against the sky and transports visitors to Fantasyland.

Below: *At night the magical Cinderella Carousel glitters with thousands of fairy lights; the giant merry-go-round with prancing horses and carriages transports Disney's guests on a journey to the ball.*

Fantasyland

Once through Sleeping Beauty Castle, complete with turrets, castellated walls and a drawbridge over a moat, one is transported into the pages of classic Disney tales. Like the magic door in *Alice in Wonderland*, the world of fairytale fantasy springs to life in the thematic rides, with a choice of a whirling ride aboard **Dumbo the Flying Elephant** to a trek through the Hundred Acre Wood in **The Many Adventures of Winnie the Pooh**. Hop on to the **Cinderella Carousel** for a ride on prancing horses in a giant merry-go-round or spin madly round on the **Mad Hatter Tea Cups** for a zany ride in giant tea cups. Immerse yourself in Disney magic in **Mickey's PhilharMagic**, a theatrical 3D adventure showcasing magical moments from classic Disney animated films, while popular and well-loved Disney characters wait to greet guests, pose for photographs and sign autographs at the **Fantasy Garden**. **Disney's Storybook Theatre** stages the 'The Golden Mickeys' at frequent intervals daily, featuring a glitzy Hollywood-style star-studded musical revue of great Disney classics such as *Mulan*, *Toy Story* and *Lilo and Stitch* among others in a 1000-seater venue. This is a good place to relax after all the exciting rides.

It's A Small World

One of the latest attractions in Fantasyland is the delightful 'It's A Small World', stationed at the fancy castle-like building with a patchwork façade of colourful panels that features the **Small World Clock Tower**. It chimes every quarter hour accompanied by a parade of Disney classic toys, with newly added Chinese opera characters for local flavour. Guests are transported on enchanted boat rides into a colourful world of joy and friendship that transcends all boundaries and nationalities as seen through the eyes of a child. The attraction is a carnival of over 400 'Audio-Animatronics' props and toy figures representing children from all over the world, dressed in their national costumes with their home country's landmarks. Each figure and prop is beautifully crafted and painted, exploding into a wonderful vibrant vision of colours and cheerfulness. Appearing in their own countries of origin are 38 Disney characters from the various Disney films and storybooks, the first time ever these characters have appeared in the 'small world' attraction anywhere in

THE ORIGINS OF DISNEYLAND®

Following a visit to Children's Fairyland in Oakland, California, with his two daughters in the 1940s, Walt Disney was inspired to build a theme park where families could spend time with their children and be entertained in a world of fairytale fantasy. He opened his first theme park, Disneyland® in Anaheim in California, on 17 July 1955. It was an immediate success. The Disney empire expanded to Florida with the opening of Walt Disney World Resort®, with the Magic Kingdom® theme park, hotel resorts, golf courses and the Experimental Prototype Community of Tomorrow (EPCOT®). Sadly Walt Disney never lived to see his Florida dream project come to fruition as he passed away on 15 December 1966 from lung cancer. His brother, Roy Disney, continued to carry out his dream until his death in 1971. Today Disney magic has expanded globally with the opening of its theme parks in France, Japan and the latest addition in Hong Kong in 2005. Walt Disney's prophesy, that 'Disneyland® will continue to grow as long as there is imagination left in this world', endures.

the world. Guests can observe Aladdin and Jasmine on their magic carpet in the Middle East scene, while Woody and Jessie from *Toy Story* make an appearance in the American scene with New York's Empire State Building and San Francisco's Golden Gate Bridge. Hong Kong Disneyland's® version of this attraction includes local elements, with scenes from famous landmarks in Hong Kong and China such as Victoria Harbour and the Star Ferry, the Great Wall of China and the Temple of Heaven. The famous catchy theme tune, *It's a Small World*, sung entirely by children, is played continuously throughout the ride in nine different languages. Four new languages exclusive to Hong Kong Disneyland® – Cantonese, Putonghua (Mandarin), Korean and Tagalog (Philippines) – are added to the five languages (English, Japanese, Italian, Spanish and Swedish) in the original version. After a hectic day at the park, this is a great ride to wind down, and the angelic voices of the children singing among the fantastic animated figures will cheer up even the most tired and cranky child or even a grumpy adult. The downside is that the theme tune will stay in your head for a while, but it's a happy tune!

Tomorrowland®

From fairytale fantasy to science fiction, Tomorrowland® propels guests to the future through space adventure in this fantastic land. For adrenalin junkies, the **Space Mountain®**, the highlight of the park, is not to be missed. It is a thrilling ride simulating a journey into space on a warp-speed roller-coaster ride into the final frontier of the universe, with cutting-edge special effects. It is not recommended for people with a nervous disposition and definitely not after a full meal. For more space experience, try the interactive **Buzz Lightyear Astro Blasters**, free-spinning Space Cruisers that take guests 'to infinity and beyond' where points can be earned zapping at comical targets with infrared laser cannons.

At the centre of the neon-lit land stands the **Orbitron**, a tower-like structure where guests can pilot colourful flying saucers on a whirling voyage through the sky. The theme park's largest restaurant, aptly named the **Starliner Diner**, provides Western fast food and refreshments.

Newer attractions here include Stitch Encounter, Autopia and UFO Zone. **Stitch Encounter** is an audience-participation experience centring around Stitch, a 'fuzzy, blue and lovable alien known officially as Experiment 626' from the 2002 Walt Disney Pictures® hit comedy *Lilo and Stitch*. Using the latest real-time computer graphics animation technology created by Walt Disney Imagineering, guests can enter the impish world of Stitch and interact with the character. The experience is conducted in Cantonese and Mandarin as well as English.

Presented by Honda, **Autopia** is a motoring attraction dubbed 'the highway of Tomorrowland®'. Guests can drive electric convertibles along winding tracks through the highways and byways of the cosmic landscape into 'alien' territory. No driver's license is required, provided guests meet the minimum height requirement of 137cm (54in) to drive alone and 81cm (32in) to ride as passengers.

UFO Zone is a delight for children and the young at heart with its 'splash-tastic' fun water games. UFO (which stands for 'Unbelievably Fun Objects') is stationed in a futuristic spaceport where various space objects – such as colourful spaceships, a water-spraying robot, water-squirting ray guns, a crashed rocket ship, flying saucer and an alien plant – will squirt and splatter water at unex-

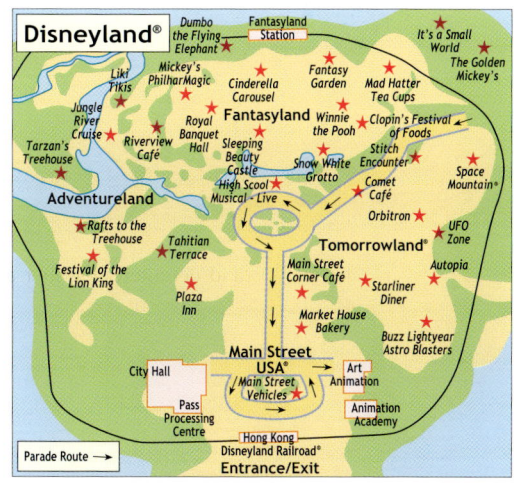

pected intervals, spraying at everyone within reach. It is a favourite with children who enjoy frolicking and playing with the water to keep cool under the hot sun.

Adventureland

Back on planet earth, you can explore the wild frontier in Adventureland on a thrilling **Jungle River Cruise**, sailing through a hostile territory with fearsome spear-wielding natives and wild animals. The boat sails through a river with whirlpools, rapids, snapping crocodiles, threatening hippos and elephants, as well as erupting volcanoes spouting molten lava. The clever electronically animated animals and characters are very life-like and add to the thrill of the river adventure. The river winds round an island with **Tarzan's Treehouse** rising high above the 'rainforest'. You can visit the treehouse by crossing the river on a raft. The main attraction here is the abridged version of the musical *Festival of the Lion King*, inspired by the Walt Disney's award-winning animated classic motion picture *The Lion King*. The colourful pageant of music and dance (with great props) is performed throughout the day in the 2250-seat **Theatre in the Wild**. Check out daily performing times at the theatre.

Below: Alice in Wonderland features in 'Disney on Parade', a sumptuous carnival procession accompanied by dancers and musicians, forming the highlight of Disneyland® where all the characters from the Disney classics come to life.

Fireworks and Parades

Aside from the thrilling rides and fun attractions, the main highlights of Disneyland® Park are '**Disney on Parade**' and '**Disney in the Stars**'. Guests are treated to a sumptuous parade at 15:30 daily – a colourful pageant of all the Disney characters on brightly coloured floats accompanied by dancers and musicians in celebration of Disney's storytelling magic through the decades. When night falls, a spectacular firework display lights up the sky, casting a magical glow on Sleeping Beauty's Castle and all the other entertainment venues in the park, accompanied by a medley of classic Disney songs. The pyrotechnical extravaganza is the climax of a visit to Disneyland® Park and is much anticipated by guests who will not leave until they have been entertained by the fireworks.

BEYOND DISNEYLAND® PARK
Inspiration Lake Recreation Centre
This lakeside park was built over an area of 30ha (74 acres) near Disneyland® Park, with an artificial 12ha (30-acre) lake used for recreation and as a reservoir for the irrigation of the entire Penny's Bay area. It is the biggest man-made lake in Hong Kong. The lake is enhanced with water cascades and a fountain spouting up to 18m (59ft) high. There are paddle boats for hire to explore the scenery around the lake, which is surrounded by a beautifully landscaped garden with a 1.5km (0.9-mile) jogging trail, exercise areas, children's playground, gazebos and a 3.5ha (8.6-acre) arboretum. Over 4800 trees and 430,000 shrubs were planted to complete the greenery. There is a boat centre and a 7-Eleven shop selling snacks and drinks. Admission to the park is free and the park opens from 09:00–19:00. It is about a 15-minute walk from Disneyland® Resort MTR, or else take the Citybus or Long Win Bus Company (bus no. R8 at Disneyland® Park) near the MTR.

Hong Kong Disneyland® Hotel
Perched right on the seafront, the Hong Kong Disneyland® Hotel is set in beautifully landscaped gardens with majestic palm trees and lush flowering plants, water features and a Mickey Mouse-shaped maze of green shrubs. The 400-room luxury hotel, reminiscent of the elegance and romance of hotels at the turn of the 20th century, is a grand Victorian design inspired by Disney's Grand Floridian Resort & Spa at Walt Disney World Resort® in Florida and at Disneyland® Paris. The sprawling six-storey resort,

DISNEY HOTELS

Disney resorts worldwide are famous for their thematic family hotels with award-winning architecture and innovative design incorporating Disney characteristics. In Hong Kong, Disney features two destination luxury hotels designed for both the family and the leisure market: **Hong Kong Disneyland® Hotel** and **Disney's Hollywood Hotel**.

featuring turrets and gabled red-shingled roofs, is set in a formal garden. The designers have added a whimsical Disney touch with their very own 'Micktorian' architecture complete with latticework, balustrades and ornate scrollwork to blend with the Victorian style but in a light, fresh colour scheme. There are many hidden Mickey Mouse images in subtle places such as on the carpet designs, buttons, dinnerware and iron railings, and it's Mickey's voice calling out the floor numbers in the lifts.

The spacious bedrooms are well equipped with a complimentary mini bar, flat-screen television, bedtime TV stories for children, wake-up calls from Mickey Mouse, complimentary high-speed Internet access and free use of the gym in the Victorian Spa. As a special gesture for families, bathrobes and slippers with the Mickey Mouse motif are provided for both adults and children, a unique feature, as most hotels normally do not provide such facilities for juvenile guests. Children can have breakfast with Disney characters.

By the entrance, two beautiful stained-glass domes preside over the grand lobby which has a nostalgic birdcage elevator to the upper floors. Staff dressed as Disney characters occasionally make appearances in the lobby to amuse the junior guests. The Grand Ballroom is decorated with 15 massive crystal and gold chandeliers, while the Grand Stair Hall features crystals in the shape of Cinderella's Glass Slipper in addition to the two crystal chandeliers overhead.

The hotel also offers corporate and convention facilities, while the formal gardens, gazebos and elegant Victorian salons are especially popular for Hong Kong Disneyland® Fairy Tale weddings.

The hotel offers an extensive programme of beauty and wellness services in its luxurious **Victorian Spa**. The spa is equipped with a whirlpool, steam room and sauna in the changing area. There is also an indoor swimming pool. Outside there is an outdoor pool and an outdoor heated whirlpool in addition to two floodlit tennis courts.

Dining Experience

There are six dining outlets in the Hong Kong Disneyland® Hotel offering a variety of cuisines from Eastern to international food and snacks.

The signature dining experience is **Crystal Lotus**, an upscale 220-seat Chinese restaurant serving the finest cuisine from major culinary regions in China. It is set in an elegant contemporary Asian decor with Chinese arts and crafts featuring crystal lotuses throughout the interior, including on the walls. Feng shui design is incorporated in the decor to create harmony by balancing the five elements of fire, water, metal, earth and wood. The water element is cleverly designed by Disney Imagineering using a computer-animated technique to create a virtual koi pond at the entrance with animated koi fish that cause ripples as they dart away when guests walk on the transparent floor. Diners can see a rock-strewn stream under the transparent floor, complete with cascading water and tropical fish.

Adjacent to the hotel lobby is the **Grand Salon** where guests can relax and enjoy afternoon tea or an evening cocktail while listening to a live orchestra, evoking an air of nostalgia for the good old days of grand high teas. The **Sorcerer's Lounge** next to the Grand Salon serves light snacks and refreshments as well as continental breakfast and high tea. The **Enchanted Garden** is set in a Victorian garden conservatory and serves a sumptuous buffet of Asian and international favourites. Disney characters make special appearances daily to join guests for breakfast and dinner. **Sea Breeze Bar**, located in a turret-shaped prime corner of the hotel by the pools, serves tropical cocktails and light Western meals and snacks. Privileged guests on the executive floors can enjoy a complimentary full American breakfast,

Below: *Hong Kong Disneyland® Hotel offers luxury accommodation in an elegant and charming atmosphere reminiscent of the grandeur of the Victorian era.*

Above: Disney's Hollywood Hotel pays tribute to the glory and glamour of Hollywood's Golden Age with show business flair.

afternoon tea and evening cocktails in the **Kingdom Club** and also be treated at night to spectacular fireworks displays from Disneyland® Park which is clearly visible from the large windows in the club.

Disney's Hollywood Hotel

Next to the Hong Kong Disneyland® Hotel is Disney's tribute to the glamour of Hollywood's Golden Age, when show business defined the era. Less grand than its sister hotel, Disney's Hollywood Hotel typifies the chic of the Art Deco architectural style, evoking the colours, texture and forms of that era, with Mickey Mouse as its signature theme. The famous motifs of Disney's iconic mouse are found everywhere, from the grand entrance to the carpet design and in the garden with Mickey Mouse park benches.

The eight-storey hotel features 600 guest rooms built in a U-shape embracing an 8ha (20-acre) palm tree-lined landscaped garden that stretches down to the South China Sea. The garden is designed with a show-business theme that unfolds like a map of the Hollywood Freeway, with the main boulevard built like a film strip branching into the famous thoroughfares of Hollywood Boulevard, Sunset Boulevard and Mullholland Drive and leading to the Hollywood Hills with its iconic word 'HOLLYWOOD' displayed boldly at the bottom of the garden. It is a favourite spot for guests to take photographs. At night, when it is lit up, the garden adds a touch of glamour to the hotel. In keeping with the showbiz theme, the outdoor swimming pool is shaped like a piano with a slide featuring 'Hidden Mickey' motifs as can be found everywhere in the hotel. There is also an outdoor heated whirlpool.

This is very much a family-oriented hotel, with a children's playground, bedtime stories and sessions with Disney characters. The facilities in the guest rooms are similar to those in its sister hotel, including bathrobes and slippers for children. The gift shop is dedicated to Disney merchandise and souvenirs.

Dining Experience

The dining outlets at Disney's Hollywood Hotel are informal to accommodate families and children. Its main restaurant, **Chef Mickey**, is kitted out with a Disney Deco style in tribute to the iconic mouse. It features a casual international buffet prepared by Disney chefs in show-kitchens with a pizza oven, a Chinese barbecue, Indian curries, Western favourites and a small à la carte menu. Children's meals are served in plastic plates and cutlery with Mickey Mouse motifs. **Hollywood and Dine** is a child-friendly eatery themed like a movie theatre lobby, with quick service for breakfast, lunch and dinner. The **Sunset Terrace** by the pool is an alfresco dining area with a barbecue, a great place to watch the sunset, while the **Piano Pool Bar** serves up tropical drinks and snacks. The indoor **Studio Lounge** is an ideal place to chill out while sipping the speciality cocktails and juices and enjoying the vista of the garden through its floor-to-ceiling windows.

NGONG PING VILLAGE ★★★

Dubbed as a 'Journey of Enlightenment', **Ngong Ping 360** is a new tourism experience with the aim of 'enlightening' guests on the spectacular 5.7km (3.5-mile) journey on the Ngong Ping Cable Car to Ngong Ping Village. The village has three cultural themes – 'Walking With Buddha', 'Monkey's Tale Theatre' and 'Ngong Ping Tea House' – to reflect and perpetuate the cultural and spiritual ethic of the Ngong Ping area. Perched on the Ngong Ping Plateau in a 1.5ha (3.7-acre) site, the village is designed in a traditional Chinese architectural style with upturned eaves on grey tile roofs and whitewashed walls, a refreshing departure

---

DISNEY MOVIES

Disney's initial foray into short animated films for Mickey and Minnie Mouse in the *Plane Crazy* and *Gallopin' Gaucho* silent films failed to attract a distributor. Undeterred, he produced his next film for Mickey Mouse called *Steamboat Willie* with a soundtrack that won instant success. His first full-length feature film, *Snow White and the Seven Dwarfs*, dubbed by his detractors as 'Disney's Folly', was premiered in 1937 to rave reviews. It was the first animated feature in English and technicolour and when it was released in February 1938, it became the most successful picture that year and reportedly earned over US$8 million in the box office and won Disney an Oscar. It set a trend for other Disney films to come. In his lifetime, he was nominated 59 times for the Academy Award and won 26 Oscars and seven Emmy awards, making him the world record holder for the most awards and nominations. The Russians even named a minor planet after him in 1980.

NGONG PING 360 GREEN CAMPAIGN

Ngong Ping 360, a subsidiary of the MTR Corporation Ltd., was officially opened on 9 November 2006. But in June 2007, when a cable car cabin was accidentally dislodged while undergoing testing, it was suspended for repair and re-opened on 31 December 2007 after all safety compliance met with current international standards. Ngong Ping 360's tagline – 'It's blue. It's green. It's love naturally' – proclaims its mission statement of 'responsible tourism development with local economic and community benefits ... firmly committed to ... sustainable development'. The cableway and stations were carefully built to minimize destruction to natural vegetation and impact on the environment. Helicopters and mules transported building materials to the North Lantau Country Park. The mules trekked up the mountain on existing footpaths to avoid having to build temporary roads. The helicopters transported over 12,000 tons of materials to the site. Unavoidable vegetation destruction was re-planted by the company. A tree-planting campaign was launched, involving staff of Ngong Ping 360 and their families along with green groups in the community. Rainwater is collected during the rainy season (Mar–Sep), stored at recycling plants at the angle stations and used for daily cleaning work.

from the typically rich multicoloured scheme of other traditional Chinese buildings in Hong Kong. The soothing colour scheme of the village blends with the tranquil greenery of the surrounding natural landscape under the shadow of the famous Tian Tan Giant Buddha. The village itself is quite limited in its attractions, but the amazing experience of getting there via the cable car is well worth the journey. It is also the gateway to the renowned Po Lin Monastery, the Giant Buddha statue and the Wisdom Path.

The village is built in a linear fashion, with the Tea House by the entrance next to the cable car station and classic Chinese-style buildings on both sides of a thoroughfare housing an array of food and beverage outlets including the ubiquitous Starbucks Coffee, which looks out of place in a Chinese village. There are souvenir shops, gifts stations and two temple-like buildings featuring the two spiritually themed attractions. The thoroughfare ends at a large gate with the characteristic of an ancient Chinese triple gateway. The path outside the village boundary leads to the Giant Buddha and Po Lin Monastery, a five-minute walk away.

The Cable Car

This is the most spectacular mode of transport to a tourist attraction in Hong Kong. The cable car journey starts from **Tung Chung Cable Car Terminal** at the new town of Tung Chung, just a few minutes' walk from the town's MTR. The gondola cableway, supported by eight towers, stretches for 5.7km (3.5 miles) with two angle stations in between, one at Airport Island and the other at Nei Lak Shan. The cable cars do not stop at these stations, which are purely for operational and emergency purposes. It is the biggest cableway in Asia and one of the most impressive ever constructed. There are 109 spacious cabins with a capacity for 17 people per cabin. The journey takes 25 glorious minutes over the stunning scenery of Lantau Island, affording a 360-degree panoramic vista of Lantau North Country Park, the South China Sea, Tung Chung Bay and Hong Kong

International Airport at Chek Lap Kok. The aerial view of North Lantau, with its magnificent mountainous terrain and sweeping spurs cloaked in verdant forest rich with over 100 species of flora, is a spectacular sight. Mountain trails, popular with hikers, can be seen snaking through the forest. As the cable cars approach Ngong Ping Village, the Tian Tan Giant Buddha looms into view among the rocky outcrops, presiding over the plateau.

Ngong Ping Tea House

For tea lovers, the Tea House is a great experience where you can learn about the culture and history of tea in Hong Kong. The Tea House, operated by **Wing Wah**, one of Hong Kong's oldest tea merchants, is established in the style of a typical Chinese inn, where guests can be educated in the tea culture through an interactive exhibition, 'The Story of Tea in Hong Kong'. The history of Hong Kong's favourite pastime of *yum cha*, the Chinese equivalent of the Western high tea, is charted in an exhibition detailing its humble beginnings in street-food stalls in the 1940s to the present-day popularity of this dining experience in modern restaurants and tea houses. *Yum cha* is a social activity where friends and families gather together for breakfast or lunch to feast on dim sum snacks washed down by copious amounts of tea. At the Tea House, Tea Masters will be on hand to demonstrate the ancient art of tea-brewing and tea appreciation. Samples of the four main varieties of home-grown Hong Kong tea – *Fung Wong* (Phoenix), originally grown on Lantau Peak, *Meng Shan* tea from Pui To Rock at Castle

Below: *Ngong Ping Tea House at Ngong Ping Village has Tea Masters at hand to demonstrate the gentle art of tea brewing and appreciation; you can learn the history of 'The Story of Tea in Hong Kong' through an interactive exhibition.*

Peak, *Daam Gon* (Shoulder Pole) tea from Tsing Yi, and *Ching Ming* (Pure Brightness) herbal tea – are introduced along with other varieties, which are brewed for guests to taste. Ngong Ping Tea House sells a wide choice of tea, Chinese teapot sets and Chinese pastries.

Walking With Buddha

Described as an 'immersive multimedia experience that explores and explains the life of Siddhartha Gautama and his path to enlightenment', this is a concise and entertaining introduction to Buddhism with a touch of contemporary showbiz gimmick. The story unfolds in seven scenes charting each stage of Siddhartha's spiritual awakening from his privileged life as a prince, heir to the kingdom of what is present-day Nepal, to his forsaking of his birthright to become a prophet. The show begins in a courtyard with an artificial Bodhi tree where, with dramatic special effect, it focuses on the stone bust of Buddha amid a cloud of mist and incense smoke. A voice representing the Spirit of the Bodhi tree narrates the story, set in a period over 2500 years ago, of a prince who was sheltered from the outside world inside the palace walls, living a life of luxury. The guests are then ushered to a theatre through a corridor of traditional flags and a Buddhist shrine and begin a journey immersed in the various stages of Siddhartha's life through animation, lighting and theatrics. Finally, having witnessed the transformation and enlightenment of the prince into Buddha through the interactive multimedia, guests are transported to stark reality in present-day Hong Kong, to a bustling scene in neon-lit Nathan Road. For the grand finale, guests enter a door to a serene temple where each one is invited to pick a plastic leaf from a basket, on which words of wisdom are inscribed, and to release the leaf inside an opaque Buddha through a slot at the seat of the statue. One can see the leaf disappearing into the Buddha, symbolic of an offering. A Zen-like path guides guests along the 'Path of Enlightenment' and on the walls are the precepts of **The Four Noble Truths**, the essence of Buddhism. When you leave the theatre into the sunlight, the vision of the Tian Tan Giant Buddha comes into view on the mountain, making the whole experience quite surreal.

Monkey's Tale Theatre

This attraction has a hint of Disney theatrics, with special effects and high-definition animation of a 'Monkey's Tale'. Guests enter the theatre under a Bodhi tree and take their seats on simulated tree trunks, with overhead projections of tree branches and leaves to give the illusion that they are sitting under the Bodhi tree. The storyline is inspired by the famous Buddhist **Jakata tales** of a selfish monkey who exploits its three monkey friends to attain a magic peach through a series of hilarious antics. Jakata folklore tends to uphold Buddhist morality, so the selfish monkey gets his karmic comeuppance and learns a powerful lesson from the Monkey King about sharing and kindness, true to the teaching of Buddha. The stage is brought to life with the animatronic monkeys and electronically controlled props and imagery. It is an enjoyable show with a moral ending.

Tian Tan Giant Buddha ***

Hailed as the biggest seated outdoor Buddha in the world, the Giant Buddha on Muk Yue Peak is the most awe-inspiring religious landmark of Hong Kong. Named after Tian Tan, the Altar of Heaven at the Temple of Heaven in Beijing, it was officially inaugurated on 29 December 1993 with much religious pomp. It is as much a religious symbol as a work of art

WORK OF WISDOM

The idea of the Wisdom Path was the brainchild of Professor Jao Tsung-I, an outstanding scholar, painter, poet and calligrapher, who presented the idea to the Hong Kong government in 2002 after seeing a Heart Sutra stone carving at Taishan in Shandong in eastern China on a visit in 1980. He created a calligraphic version of the text and donated it to the people of Hong Kong. The professor's works are internationally renowned and the government tasked the Tourism Commission to transform his calligraphy into a living artwork, calling it 'The Wisdom Path'. It has profound meaning to followers of Buddhism and the park is a mecca for devotees as well as tourists. For a worthwhile day excursion, it is recommended to combine the visit with Ngong Ping Village, the Giant Buddha and Po Lin Monastery.

Right: *An ornate temple in the Po Lin Monastery complex, one of the biggest places of worship in Hong Kong. It is famed for its Giant Buddha situated on a hill top facing the monastery.*

in bronze inspired by art work from the Sui and Tang dynasties. It is made up of 202 pieces of bronze, cast in China and welded together on site, and weighs 250 tons. The magnificent sculpture is in the image of **Amitabha Buddha** seated in a lotus position on a lotus throne perched on a $2239m^2$ (24,100-sq-ft) three-storey pedestal. It sits atop the peak, presiding over Po Lin Monastery with the mountains and sea beyond, facing northeast towards Beijing. The statue, together with the pedestal, measures 34m (112ft) high and houses the Hall of Benevolent Merit, Hall of Universe and Memorial Hall. There are two relics, the size of a grain of rice each, of Gautama Buddha's remains, enshrined in the Memorial Hall on the third floor.

In the foyer of the pedestal leading to the three halls is a huge bell weighing 6 tons with a 2m (6.6ft) diameter, engraved with images of Buddha in various *mudra* along with Buddhist scriptures. It is programmed by a computer to ring 108 times per day to symbolize the eradication of humans' 108 worldly tribulations according to Buddhist belief. The Giant Buddha is accessed via 268 steps and the view at the peak is breathtaking. Basking under the shadow of the Giant Buddha surrounded by statues of eight immortals, it is well worth the ascent.

Po Lin Monastery ★★★

In 1906 three Zen monks – named Da Yue, Dun Xiu and Yue Ming – from Jin Shan Monastery in Zhejiang, an eastern coastal province in China, came to Ngong Ping and built a small monastery comprising just a modest stone house and a big hut. Soon the sacred place became well known in the region and more monks came to join them. The monastery was simply called 'The Big Hut'. Its name was changed to Po Lin, meaning 'Precious Lotus' in Chinese, when Venerable Jin Xiu, a senior monk from the same monastery in China, became the first abbot at the temple in 1924. From 1928 onwards, more buildings were built as the monastery became more established. Today Po Lin Monastery is a religious complex of several ornate temples and halls nestled between Lantau Peak and Lei Nak Shan overlooked by the Giant Buddha up the hill.

The principal features of the monastery are set in a serene landscape with tree-lined avenues and gardens bursting with the purple blooms of the bougainvillaea and other flowering shrubs. The entrance is marked by the bronze cauldron (*see* panel, this page) and a three-tier circular platform called **Tei Tan**, modelled after the Tian Tan at the Temple of Heaven in Beijing. Next to the structure is an imposing memorial gate built in a classic Chinese style with three gateways. Just inside the compound is the **Welto Temple**, dedicated to the guardian of the Hall of Hero. This immortal is accompanied by the four 'Heavenly Kings' who guard the four corners of the earth from evil.

Behind the Welto Temple, separated from it by a square, is the **Hall of Great Hero** (more popularly known as the 'Big Temple') – the heart of the monastery where the three main Buddha statues are housed. It was completed in 1970 in the grand style of a classic Chinese imperial temple, characterized by a double-tier roof elaborately decorated with mythical animals. A row of pillars intricately engraved with swirling dragons on clouds supports the structure. A flight of steps protected by a pair of temple lions leads to the main hall,

THE CAULDRON OF PO LIN MONASTERY

One of the notable features of the monastery is a massive bronze cauldron on a pedestal standing in the square at the entrance in alignment with the Giant Buddha. It was installed on New Year's Eve in 1998 to commemorate the return of sovereignty of Hong Kong to China the year before. The cauldron with the pedestal stands at 4.1m (13.5ft) high and weighs 5000kg (11,025lb) in total. The outer wall of the cauldron is engraved with the **bauhinia**, the emblem of Hong Kong, while the main precepts of the **Basic Law** of the country are inscribed in the inner wall to mark its importance in history.

lavishly decorated in the auspicious colours of mainly red and gold with sumptuous lanterns, religious hangings and bunting festooned from the ceiling. The main altar, loaded with votive offerings, is consecrated with three exquisite golden Buddha statues – in the middle sits **Sakyamuni Buddha**, representing the present, flanked on the left by the **Medicine Buddha** of the past, while **Amitabha**, the Buddha of the future, occupies the right-hand side. Two of Buddha's ten principal attendants, **Kassapa** and **Anan**, stand on either side of Sakyamuni Buddha. This is one of the most exquisitely decorated temples in Hong Kong.

Behind the temple is the **Scripture Library** where all the sacred texts and sutras are kept. If spiritual enlightenment after the visit does not stave off hunger, the monastery restaurant is a great pit stop for vegetarian food and dessert for which the monastery is renowned.

The Wisdom Path **

Below: *The Wisdom Path illustrates the Buddhist Heart Sutra on giant wooden columns, arranged in a figure eight to symbolize infinity, set on a scenic hill at the foot of the Lantau Peak.*

In keeping with the spiritual theme of the Ngong Ping Plateau tourist attractions, the Wisdom Path is, in effect, the Heart Sutra, literally set in wood (*see* panel, page 107). The Wisdom Path is a park set at the foot of picturesque Lantau Peak, with an outdoor exhibition of giant timber columns inscribed with verses from the holy text in Chinese calligraphy. There are 38 columns rising up to about 10m (33ft) high, arranged in a figure eight to symbolize infinity. They are erected in harmony with the contour of the hill, with footpaths following the configuration. At the highest point of the hill, a pillar has been left blank to denote the concept of 'emptiness', the central theme of the Heart Sutra. Visitors can stroll through the park among the wooden pillars while

at the same time enjoying the wild beauty of Lantau Peak. The Wisdom Path display is akin to the religious texts written on bamboo tablets in ancient times, created here into outdoor monumental art.

The park is about 15 minutes' walk from Po Lin Monastery through a pleasant forest path. The gentle slope of the hill up Wisdom Path makes it an easy climb and there is a pavilion at the entrance to the park where you can have a rest stop and soak up the peaceful ambience.

Tai O Village *

This fishing village on the northwest coast of Lantau is one of the few remaining coastal villages in Hong Kong. Tai O was reputedly once a hideout where pirates found safe harbour in the sheltered coves. It is situated on a small island at the confluence of a river, linked to the mainland via a pedestrian drawbridge. The time-warp village is home to the Tanka people who live in rustic wooden houses built on stilts over the tidal mud flats. They were pioneers from China who settled in Hong Kong. Their main livelihood is fishing and selling fish products such as salted fish, fish maws and shrimp paste in the local markets by the seafront. These food delicacies are staples in some Chinese cuisines. In China the Tanka people traditionally live in boats, but the fishing community here live in coastal villages perched by the sea. The population is slowly diminishing as the educated younger generation tend to move away to urban areas to look for employment.

Places of interest include a few Chinese temples and the market. The ferry pier is a great place to watch the sunset. It is feasible to include Tai O in the itinerary with Ngong Ping Village and Po Lin Monastery. There is a bus service near Po Lin Monastery to Tai O Village which takes about 20 minutes. If travelling from Hong Kong Island, take the ferry from Central Pier 6 to Mui Wo and transfer to bus no. 1 to Tai O. Alternatively you can go to Tung Chung MTR and take bus no. 11 from Tung Chung town centre.

THE HEART SUTRA

The Heart Sutra is the shortest presentation of the practice of **Prajna Paramita Hrdaya Sutra**, the perfection of wisdom in Buddhism. Its concise text of 260 words basically articulates the doctrine of 'emptiness' which preaches non-attachment to material things in order to obtain an unobstructed mind and discover the path of enlightenment. It is one of the central texts of **Mahayana Buddhism**, treasured by Buddhists, Taoist and Confucian alike. It is central to the teaching of Buddha and is chanted daily in temples, monasteries and centres around the world.

7. Lamma Island, Cheung Chau and Macau

LAMMA ISLAND **

Lamma Island is the third largest island in Hong Kong, with a landmass of 13.55km² (5.2 sq miles). It is situated southwest from Hong Kong Island, separated by the East Lamma Channel. Lamma Island's claim to fame is the famous actor **Chow Yun-Fat** who was born and raised here. The island has a Y-shaped outline and a craggy coastline punctuated with sandy coves. The interior is hilly, with the highest peak rising to 353m (1158ft) at **Mount Stenhouse**. Early historic records indicate that the island was a stopover for merchant vessels en route to Guangzhou for trade during the 6th century. Its rustic character is like a throwback of Hong Kong before it became a thoroughly modern city-state. Just half an hour from Hong Kong Island, it is like stepping back in time to an island that manages to escape the clutches of urban development. The natural beauty embracing the whole island in a village setting inspires an unhurried pace, perfect for a break from the pulsating metropolis and traffic. The absence of high-rise buildings and cars is like stepping onto a different planet and is eerily unreal if you have just stepped off the ferry from Hong Kong Island. Buildings are all low rise and there are no big roads as the only motor traffic allowed on the island are service vehicles such as ambulances, fire engines and vans for transporting goods and utility products. The only mode of transport on the island is by bicycle or on foot. With its close proximity to the city, it is a favourite island getaway for

DON'T MISS

** **Yung Shue Wan:** the gateway to Lamma, with a scenic coastal walk.
** **Sok Kwu Wan:** rustic fishing village where you can savour the local ambience.
** **Rainbow Seafood Restaurant:** great seafood.
** **Lamma Fisherfolk's Village:** a showcase of the fishing culture.
** **Macau:** a taste of Portuguese culture in a Chinese city.

Opposite: *Yung Shue Wan, the main port of call at Lamma Island, still maintains a close-knit community.*

CHOW YUN-FAT, LAMMA'S 'HIDDEN DRAGON'

Chow Yun-Fat was born on Lamma Island on 18 May 1955 from a humble Hakka background. The family moved to Kowloon when he was 10 and he left school at 17, working in odd jobs to help support the family. He enrolled as a trainee actor at the TVB, Hong Kong's most powerful television station. Upon graduation a year later, he was given a three-year contract with TVB. His debut leading role in a movie came in 1981 when he starred in *The Bund* and became a household name in Southeast Asia. In 1985, he won the Best Actor Award at the Hong Kong Academy Awards for his role in John Woo's film, *A Better Tomorrow*. International fame came in the Academy Award-winning film, *Crouching Tiger, Hidden Dragon*, directed by the renowned director Ang Lee, co-starring with Michelle Yeoh, one of Hong Kong's leading actresses. He also played the King in *Anna and The King*, co-starring with Jodie Foster. Since then he has starred in a number of Hollywood films and in 2007 he was cast in *Pirates of the Caribbean: At World's End* as a Chinese pirate leader based on Hong Kong's notorious pirate Cheung Po Tsai who used to rule the sea around Stanley in the 19th century. From Lamma Island to Hollywood, Chow Yun-Fat's meteoric rise to fame is the pride of the island.

city dwellers and has attracted a large community of expatriates and local middle-class people as residents; they find the idyllic lifestyle in a cleaner, quieter environment more attractive than life in the city. The laid-back atmosphere, surrounded by unspoilt natural beauty, is a magnet for people who lead free-spirited Bohemian lifestyles – artists, musicians, actors, new-age followers and nature lovers have adopted the island as their home. Rent, property prices and the cost of living are lower than in Hong Kong proper.

The island has a population of about 6000, residing mostly in **Yung Shue Wan** in the north and **Sok Kwu Wan** in the east. There is a picturesque hilly path linking the two villages that takes over an hour to hike but is best to take at a leisurely pace to enjoy the sights en route and relax on the beach on the way. There are pavilions off the track where you can rest and admire the sea view flanked by sweeping mountain spurs and valleys. Strange rock formations sculpted by nature are dotted along the coast. Near the villages, drink and snack kiosks provide refreshment along the way. There are several hiking trails snaking up the mountains that seem to attract the city slickers at weekends to pump up their adrenaline by scaling up the dizzy heights for a respite from their hectic urban lifestyle. Scenic spots and villages are well signposted.

Yung Shue Wan **
Located on the northern shore of the island, Yung Shue Wan, or Banyan Tree Bay, is the main port of call from Hong Kong Island. It is the most populated part of the island, with a mixture of indigenous residents and outsiders from the city including a large community of expatriates. The narrow **Main Street** runs through the village, with rows of seafood restaurants, pubs, bakeries and cafés. There are shops selling Oriental handicrafts, clothes and new-age products like incense, scented candles and aromatherapy essential oils. Stalls selling beachwear, beach balls and tacky souvenirs line the street. It is a bustling village, thronged with locals and tourists.

For peace and quiet, head out of the village in the direction of Sok Kwu Wan to enjoy the country-side. Take time to stroll through the wild flora, with birds and butterflies fluttering among the shrubs on the mountain view side of the path, while the coastal vista affords a distant hazy view of Hong Kong Island and the shimmering waters of the South China Sea, dotted with fishing boats, ferries and yachts.

Above: *Hung Shing Ye Beach on Lamma Island is the most popular beach on the island, with a safety net boundary in the water, a lifeguard on duty and facilities for showers and barbecues.*

On the way, there are promontories with jagged rocks petering out into the sea that make excellent places for photography and a rest. Stalls selling snacks and drinks are strategically placed along these scenic routes. Along the way to the eastern shore, there are some villages with ramshackle dwellings, some selling local drinks and desserts. Narrow lanes lead to private homes branching off the main road into private gardens. Shrines with votive offerings for the Earth God are set up under a tree or a street corner. Among these rustic village scenes, Hong Kong Island and Kowloon seem a million miles away.

Just round the bay south of Yung Shue Wan, the road passes a stretch of powdery sand at **Hung Shing Ye Beach**. It is the most popular beach on Lamma Island due to its proximity to the village. The water is clean and it is classified as a Grade 1 beach, with safety net boundary and lifeguards on duty. There are refresh-ment kiosks and barbecue pits, some with a strange sign that says 'No smoking at barbecue pit'. Showers and changing rooms are available for swimmers. The beach is usually very crowded at weekends and on public holidays. The tranquil scenery round the corner

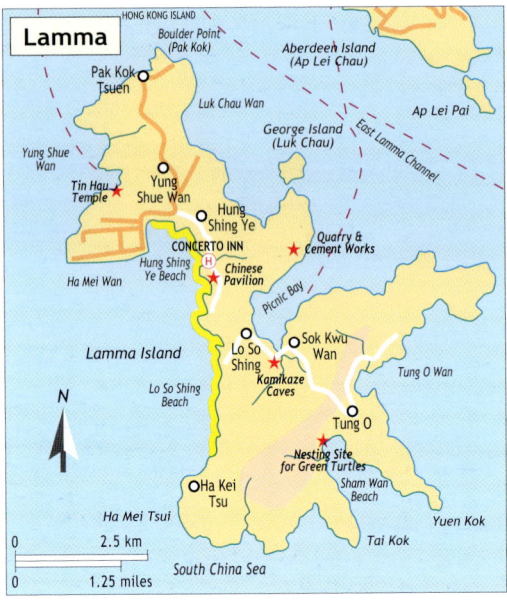

from the beach is shattered by three giant chimney stacks billowing smoke in the wind. This inevitable eyesore belongs to the Hong Kong Electric power station which supplies most of the electricity for Lamma and also Hong Kong Island.

Sok Kwu Wan ★★

From Yung Shue Wan, take the signposted **Family Trail** to the eastern coast to reach the village of Sok Kwu Wan. This fishing village is the second largest settlement on Lamma Island. Along the way, there is more stunning scenery – shrublands, bamboo groves and fishermen's homes. Near the village are rock faces pockmarked with caves signposted 'Kamikaze Caves'. These are reputedly the remnants of the Japanese occupation during the war, when they used to dig out caves from the rocks to store their boats and ammunition. The caves look forbidding, abandoned and overgrown with plants, and are sinister reminder of the atrocities of the war. Just before you reach the village, there is a pretty Chinese-style pavilion with red pillars and a green roof with upturned eaves, situated right on a headland overlooking Sok Kwu Wan. It is worth stopping here for an overview of the village, the only coastal village in Hong Kong that preserves the culture and history of the fishing industry. Wooden buildings built on stilts line the shore, with a plethora of seafood restaurants and shops selling dried seafood products and shrimp paste. The seafood is alive and swimming in fish tanks and diners can pick their 'victims' for the pot. The most popular restaurant here is **Rainbow Seafood Restaurant** which offers a free ferry shuttle for their patrons from Hong Kong Island and Kowloon. The sheltered water around the village is inundated with floating fish farms on rafts, used to breed fish for the market and restaurants.

Just before the seafood promenade stands a **Tin Hau Temple** built in 1826 (the same year as the Tin Hau Temple in Yung Shue Wan). It was destroyed by a fire in 2004 and rebuilt in 2005. The temple, dedicated to the Goddess of the Sea, is ubiquitous in every fishing village in Hong Kong to protect the seafaring community. The small temple has an imposing red door with images of the two heavenly guardians in addition to a pair of stone temple lions guarding the temple gate. In front of the temple is a big square, with two additional stone lions facing the sea for protection from malevolent spirits. The square is used for religious festivals and celebrations. Tin Hau Festival is usually celebrated by the fishing community, with fervour and religious ceremony, around April or May, depending on the lunar calendar. The festival features Cantonese opera, floats and lion dances.

Lo So Shing Beach on the eastern coast near Sok Kwu Wan is a quieter beach due to its remote location. The sandy beach is also classified as a Grade 1 beach, with clean water, showers, changing facilities and refreshment kiosks.

Not far from the village, on the southern tip of the island, is **Sham Wan Beach**, famous for its archaeological sites which trace human settlement in the northern and eastern part of the island to about 1600BC in the Neolithic and Bronze ages. It is also the nesting site for green turtles. Apart from the green turtles, hawksbill, olive ridley and leatherback turtles are found in the waters of Hong Kong, but only the green turtles have been observed nesting at Sham Wan Beach. Although sightings are getting rarer, they have been seen nesting in recent years. The nesting site covers an area of 5100m² (1.26 acres). The beach is closed to the

LAMMA FISHERFOLK'S VILLAGE

The fishing industry plays an important role in the history of Hong Kong, which itself started as a small fishing village. The Lamma Fisherfolk's Village pays tribute to the history and culture of the industry at Sok Kwu Wan Bay. Set on a floating platform complex of 2000m² (21,528 sq ft), the village comprises an exhibition hall showcasing the daily life of the floating community in fishing villages, traditional dragon boats, themed folklore booths, fishing rafts and an authentic traditional junk that houses a typical home of a fisherman and his family. There are interactive activities with demonstrations of fishing methods, while fishermen show off the skill and tricks of the trade. There are a tea house and snack bars for refreshment. The Lamma Fisherfolk's Village provides a free boat transfer from Sok Kwu Wan to the attraction, about two minutes' ride. Opening times are 10:00–19:00, website: www.fisherfolks.com.hk

public during the nesting season between June and October. To get there, take a ferry service to Yung Shue Wan or Sok Kwu Wan (about 30 minutes) from Central Pier 4 (Hong Kong MTR/Airport Express Exit E1). Rainbow Seafood Restaurant offers a free ferry shuttle to its restaurant at Sok Kwu Wan from Central Pier 9 and Kowloon Public Pier, with prior reservation.

CHEUNG CHAU *

Sandwiched between Lantau and Lamma islands, Cheung Chau lies 11km (7 miles) southwest from Hong Kong Island and is the most densely populated of all the outlying islands, with a population of more than 30,000 including expatriates who have settled on the island. Its topography is made up of two hilly granite masses joined together by a stretch of sandy causeway, giving it the shape of a dumbbell. Its name in Cantonese means 'Long Island' and its total landmass of 2.45km² (1 sq mile) is fringed by rugged coastline harbouring eight sandy bays. The main bay is at **Tung Wan Beach** opposite the ferry pier. The main settlement is centred round the causeway with its sheltered bays and low elevation. The town is traversed with narrow streets that do not accommodate motor traffic, except 'Village Vehicles' which are service vehicles for ambulance, fire engine, police and utility transport. The natives of Cheung Chau are of the dialect groups of Huizhou, Chaozhou (a.k.a. Chiu Chow) and Guangzhou from the Guangdong and Fujian provinces in southern China whose main livelihood was fishing. Today the fishing community still thrives and the island's economy has extended to commerce and tourism.

Cheung Chau's claim to fame is **Lee Lai Shan**, the first gold medallist in windsurfing for Hong Kong in the 1996 Olympics. Affectionately known as San San, Lee was born in Cheung Chau on 5 September 1970. She started windsurfing at the age of 12 under the tutorship of her uncle who still runs the **Windsurfing Centre** on the island. She joined the Hong Kong team at the age of 19 and went on to win the gold medal in windsurfing for Hong Kong. She was the first and last athlete ever to win a medal in the Olympics under the British rule. In 2008, she had the honour of being the first person to carry the Olympic torch on the torch relay leg in Hong Kong and was the final torch bearer at the summer Olympic sailing ceremony at Qingdao International Marina.

Bun Festival **

The islanders still observe age-old traditions of religious festivals and the island is synonymous with the Bun

Festival, known in Chinese as 'Tai Ping Qing Jiao' or 'Purest sacrifice celebrated for great peace', which is held every May. The festival is said to have started when the island was devastated by a plague outbreak in 1777 and the local people beseeched the help of Pak Tai, a deity known as the 'Supreme Emperor of the Dark Heaven', who is known for his power to dispel disasters. The Huizhou took the image of Pak Tai from their native county to Cheung Chau and the plague was suppressed; since then peace descended on the island. The islanders proclaimed Pak Tai the patron saint of the island and a temple was built in his honour in 1783 by the Huizhou.

Every year in May, before the fishing season begins, Cheung Chau celebrates a thanksgiving festival in Pak Tai's honour by having a three-day ritualistic celebration with parades of the deities and a carnival of lion dance, Cantonese operas, a float procession in which children aged between five and eight are hoisted on frames a few metres in the air, dressed in costumes representing historical and mythological figures and accompanied by throngs of crowds through the streets.

Above: *The annual Bun Festival, with its towers of bun offerings to the 'hungry ghosts' and its ritualistic 'bun fights', is a major event both for the islanders and visitors in Cheung Chau.*

Cheung Chau

Chi Ma Wan Peninsula

HONG KONG ISLAND

Lantau

Cheung Chau

Tung Wan Tsai

MACAU

Tai Kwai Wan

Pak Tai Temple

Tung Wan Beach

Cheung Chau Village

Kwun Yam Wan

Kwun Yam Wan Beach

Boatyards

Cheung Chau Wan

Ferry Pier

Windsurfing Centre

Kwum Yam Wan Temple

Vase Rock

Human Head Rock

Nam Tam

Fa Peng

Sai Wan

Lung Tsai Tsuen

Nam Tam Wan

Cheung Po Tsai Cave

Cheung Chau Meteorological Station

Pak Tso Wan

Italian Beach

South China Sea

N

0   5 km

0   2.5 miles

Musicians bang their gongs and drums loudly to ward off evil spirits. It is said that the island used to be plagued by pirates who would massacre the natives, and the festival is also to appease the wandering spirits of the dead. The highlight of the festival, which takes place outside the Pak Tai Temple, is the 'bun fight' ceremony in which three giant bamboo towers of some 18m (60ft) tall are plastered with steamed buns as offerings to the hungry ghosts. Three designated climbers clamber up the towers to retrieve as many buns as possible to be distributed to the villagers. The higher the buns on the tower, the more luck they will bring, so the task is to climb right up to the top. It used to be a free-for-all scramble for the bun tower until a tower collapsed in 1978, injuring over a hundred people. The government banned the practice until 2004 when the tradition was revived but under the scrutiny of the government's health and safety regulations. It has become a spectator sport for visitors. At the expense of age-old tradition, the bun tower is now a 14m-tall (46ft) steel tower covered with symbolic plastic buns, as real steamed buns left on the tower for three days are now deemed unhygienic by the authorities. Twelve climbers are selected from well-trained athletes and they climb the towers, with special harnesses for safety, in a competition to gather as many buns as possible. The Bun Festival is a major tourist attraction and thousands flock to the island during this period.

Coastal Walks *

Aside from the festival, Cheung Chau's coastal terrain offers great hiking trails along the southeast coast with its scenic 'Mini Great Wall' walk – not quite a wall but an undulating path with white paving stones. It weaves up and down the hilly terrain leading to some strange rock formations nicknamed 'Flower Vase', 'The Bell' and 'Human Head' due to their resemblance to these objects – with a bit of embellishment imagination. The southwest coast is no less picturesque, with its wild beauty, and the most popular attraction here is the **Cheung Po Tsai Cave**, reputedly used by an infamous 19th-century pirate to hide his loot. Make sure you are equipped with a torch before exploring the cave.

Pak Tai Temple **

Other attractions on the island are the many old temples dedicated to the various deities, notably the Pak Tai Temple, the centre of the Bun Festival celebration. Built in 1783, the temple has gone through many renovations over the centuries and it has been listed as a Grade 1 historical building by the Antiquities Advisory Committee. Located on the main street at Pak She Street, it is built in the traditional Chinese temple architecture with an ornate façade and lavish interior. Pak Tai is the main deity, complemented by Tai Sui, 'the Sixty Heavenly Generals of Time' (the keepers of the Chinese zodiac's 60-year cycle) and Kwun Yum (a.k.a. Kwan Yin), the Goddess of Mercy. The temple is a treasure trove of antiques, including a big sword from the Song Dynasty (960–1279); a wooden sedan chair made in 1894; an 1861 stone cauldron; two granite pillars engraved with dragons installed in 1903; and a golden crown donated by a worshipper in honour of the official visit of the late Princess Margaret and the Earl of Snowdon in 1966. The temple is open from 07:00 to 17:00.

To get to Cheung Chau, take the ferry from Central Pier 5 (Hong Kong MTR/Airport Express Exit E1) in Central. On Saturdays, Sundays and public holidays

PAK TAI, SUPREME EMPEROR OF THE DARK HEAVEN

Legend has it that Pak Tai (a.k.a. Bei Di) was a prince from the Shang Dynasty and was appointed commander of the 12 heavenly legions by the Jade Emperor to defeat the Demon King who was rampaging through the region during the fall of the Shang Dynasty. The Demon King, accompanied by a tortoise and a serpent, went to battle, was defeated by Pak Tai and banished. For his valour and victory, Pak Tai was bestowed the title 'Supreme Emperor of the Dark Heaven' and 'Supreme Emperor of the North'. He was known to be the destroyer of evil and protector of seafarers. His statue is portrayed with a tortoise and serpent trodden under his feet to symbolize good triumphant over evil. He is the patron saint of Cheung Chau.

THE PORTUGUESE

Portuguese is still one of the official languages of Macau, besides Cantonese and Mandarin, although English is still the language used in trade and tourism. Signs and notices appear in Portuguese alongside Chinese and English, but in reality only a handful of the population can speak or read Portuguese, and these are mostly to be found among the older generation.

GETTING TO MACAU

There are several services to Macau from Hong Kong at frequent intervals. **Turbojet** leaves from the Hong Kong-Macau Ferry Terminal at Shun Tak Centre at Sheung Wan in Hong Kong Island, tel: 852 2921 6688, www.turbojet.com.hk The journey takes an hour. **First Ferry** leaves from China (HK) Ferry Terminal in Tsim Sha Tsui, tel: 852 2526 9581, www.nwff.com.hk The journey takes 60–75 minutes. **Cotai Strip CotaiJet** leaves from the Hong Kong-Macau Ferry Terminal to Taipa Ferry Terminal, tel: 852 2359 9990, www.cotaijet.com.mo The journey takes an hour.

there are services from Tsim Sha Tsui at Star Ferry Pier via Mui Wo in Lantau Island. The ferry service is operated by New World First Ferry. For the current schedule and fares, log on to www.nwff.com.hk

EXCURSION TO MACAU **

For a historical jaunt with a Portuguese flavour and a dice with lady luck at the casinos, an excursion to Macau makes an interesting day trip from Hong Kong. This small but very wealthy special administrative region of China enjoys the same political autonomy as Hong Kong under the 'One Country, Two Systems' rule as the **Macau Special Administrative Region**. It is the first and last vestige of European colonization in China; the Portuguese first set foot on it in the 16th century and stayed until the handover over to China on 20 December 1999, two years after Hong Kong.

The Macau Peninsula is situated 60km (37 miles) southwest of Hong Kong at the mouth of the western side of the Pearl River Delta, bordering Guangdong Province in the north and surrounded by the South China Sea in the south and east. It has a total area of 29.2km^2 (11.3 sq miles), with a population of 557,400 comprising 95% Chinese, the rest coming from Hong Kong and other countries. Macau consists of the **Macau Peninsula**, the islands of **Taipa** and **Coloane**, and the 5.6km^2 (2-sq-mile) reclaimed strip of **Cotai** in between the two islands, named after the amalgamation of the first few letters of Coloane and Taipa. There are three bridges linking Macau to Taipa. Due to its geographical location, when it was part of the Silk Road trading route for loading silk en route to Europe its original name was 'Ou Mun' or 'Trading Gate'. The first known settlers were mainly fishermen from the Fujian Province and farmers from Guangdong. In the 1550s the Portuguese arrived and, upon landing in Macau, they asked the name of the port and were told by the locals that it was called 'A-Ma Gao' or 'the place of A-Ma', which was the name of a temple built here in honour of the Goddess of the Sea (also known as Matzu or Tin Hau, depending on the Chinese dialects). The Portuguese decided to adopt the name and named it Macau, though it is still known as 'Ou Mun' among the Chinese today. The Portuguese set up a colony with consent from China and it developed into a thriving entrepôt between East and West. The Portuguese ruled Macau for 400 years and left behind an indelible legacy in the social and cultural heritage of the country. Today Macau's main economic activities are banking, manufacturing of textiles, electronics and toys, as well as tourism – notably the gambling industry.

Macau in a Day

The main tourist attractions can be found around the **Historic Centre**, listed as a World Heritage Site by UNESCO on 15 July 2005, the 31st site in China to be granted this status. It covers eight squares and 22 historic buildings. The Portuguese legacy blends harmoniously with the Chinese heritage, weaving a fascinating tapestry of a living culture. The historic architecture and structure of the city are mainly Portuguese, with some Eastern touches, and interspersed between the European buildings are Chinese temples and mansions.

The heritage trail is best explored on foot. Start at the **A-Ma Temple** where it all began 400 years ago when the Portuguese first came to Macau in 1557. The Chinese agreed to let the Portuguese colonize the peninsula in exchange for clearing the surrounding sea of marauding pirates. The ancient temple is dedicated to A-Ma, the Sea Goddess. Legend has it that A-Ma started life as a mortal. One day she was looking for a passage to

Above: *The historical façade of St Paul's Church, a heritage from its Portuguese legacy, is the most famous landmark in Macau.*

Canton but was turned down by wealthy junk owners until a poor fisherman offered her a ride. During the journey, a violent stormed destroyed all the other junks except the fisherman's boat. When they reached Macau, the young girl vanished and returned as an immortal and is worshipped as the protector of fishermen.

Painted in an auspicious red colour with a very ornate roof and a façade engraved with Chinese mythological and religious motifs, the temple is built on a small hillock facing the sea. The temple has pavilions, gardens and prayer halls festooned with large coiled incense suspended from the ceiling. At the entrance of the temple is a large rock with a carving of a traditional sailing junk engraved over 400 years ago to denote its seafaring status. Boulders around the temple compound are etched with red 'good luck' Chinese calligraphy. Near the temple is **Pastelaria Koi Kei**, a large shop selling delicious Chinese snacks, barbecue pork and egg tarts, the signature pastry of Macau.

Below: *The Grand Lisboa, an ultra swanky and conspicuous hotel and casino, shaped like a glittering lotus, dominates the skyline of Macau.*

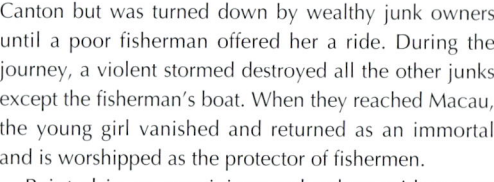

The most famous landmark of Macau is the magnificent façade of the ruins of **St Paul's Church**. It was built in 1602 but was destroyed by fire in 1835 and all that remains is the imposing façade with a grand staircase sweeping down to the heart of the city. The colonnaded façade is intricately carved with European motifs featuring a touch of the East. It has several alcoves decorated with religious statues. It is a reminder of the grandeur of the golden age under the Portuguese rule when many grand buildings were built.

Just behind St Paul's is the **Na Tcha Chinese Temple**,

looking somewhat incongruous next to such an imposing European structure. This illustrates the perfect integration of the two cultures. The temple is dedicated to the child god Na Tcha, a god noted for his mischief and filial devotion to his parents. The modest temple was built in 1888 to appeal to Na Tcha to stop the plague outbreak at the time. Alongside the temple is a section of the old city wall built by the Portuguese in 1569 and completed in 1632 as part of the fortresses and city walls surrounding the then inner harbour west of Macau. A short walk from here leads to the heart of the city at **Senado Square**.

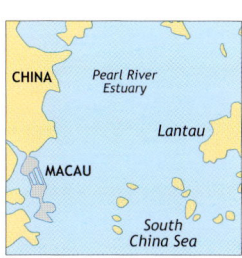

This beautiful square is a living museum of the Portuguese colony, with many historical buildings all preserved in their former glory. The square is paved in mosaic with wavy designs in alternate colours of black and white to symbolize the maritime heritage of the Portuguese. Hence this square is also known as the 'Maritime Square', with a fountain topped by a globe to indicate the sea voyages of the pioneering Portuguese. It is a bustling shopping district with modern brand names alongside great heritage buildings, notably the **St Dominic Church** and the **Leal Senado** building, which is an outstanding example of Portuguese architecture, used today as a municipal chamber with the ground floor dedicated to a gallery and the first floor to a public library. The beautiful cream and white St Dominic Church has an impressive façade embellished with stucco moulding and green shuttered windows. The bell tower at the back of the church houses a museum of 'Treasures of Sacred Art'. The serene interior of the church belies its violent historical past, involving the murder of a military officer in 1644 at the altar during Mass because of his support of the Spanish against the Portuguese. It was also the scene of a violent conflict in 1707 between the Dominicans and the authorities, when the friars sided with the Pope against the Bishop of Macau over the Rites Controversy. Other notable historic places are the plethora of churches, temples and elegant squares around the Historic Centre.

GAMBLING

Macau is synonymous with casinos and has been dubbed the 'Las Vegas of the East', with famous names from 'Sin City' such as MGM Grand Paradise, Sands, Wynn and Venetian now branching into Macau. The Grand Lisboa is probably one of the most outstanding and swankiest hotels in the city, shaped like a golden lotus sprouting into the sky. Even if you are not a gambler, it is worth visiting these grand hotels, with their sumptuous and opulent decor, just to experience their decadence. There are numerous casinos in the city and they are known to offer the widest range of games in the world. They are open 24 hours a day and most of them offer free shuttle bus services from the Macau Ferry Terminal. Hong Kong currency is accepted in Macau.

Travel Tips

Best Time to Visit

Hong Kong is an all-year destination with a subtropical climate but the most pleasant time to visit is **Nov–Dec** when the weather is sunny with comfortable temperatures and very low humidity.

Visitor Information

There are three **HKTB Visitor Information & Services Centres** at the **airport** – at Transfer Area E2 and Buffer Hall A & B at Arrival Level Terminal 1. Service hours are 07:00–23:00. **Visitor Hotline** (multilingual), tel: 852 2508 1234 (09:00–18:00 daily). The **city offices** are at Star Ferry Concourse at Tsim Sha Tsui (08:00–20:00), Causeway Bay MTR near Exit F (08:00–20:00) and the Peak Piazza, between the Peak Tower and the Peak Galleria (09:00–21:00).

Entry Requirements

Visitors must hold valid passports. Visitors from most countries do not require a visa and can stay from seven days to 180 days depending on nationality. For visa information, check on the Hong Kong Immigration Department website (www.immd.gov.hk) or at any Chinese consular mission in your home country.

Customs Allowance

Visitors aged 18 or above may bring into Hong Kong one litre of liquor, 60 cigarettes or 15 cigars or 75 grams of other manufactured tobacco. All other consumer goods in Hong Kong are duty free and without restriction. For further details, check on www.customs.gov.hk

Accommodation

Hong Kong offers accommodation to suit all budgets with more than 50,000 rooms available. For the well-heeled and corporate travellers, the **ultra luxury hotels** are second to none, with every facility for business or pleasure. All are wired up with the latest technology and also have amenities for serious pampering. Award-winning restaurants provide a delightful gourmet experience, catering for even the most discerning epicureans. In the **four-star** or **boutique hotels**, the accommodation may be less luxurious but is equally comfortable with almost the same facilities. For budget travellers, **guesthouses** and **hostels** offer affordable accommodation (in less salubrious surroundings) with very compact rooms and limited but adequate facilities. Most have air conditioning and *en-suite* showers or bathroom. It is advisable to stay in government licensed guesthouses (www.hadla.gov.hk/english). **Youth hostels** are ideal for young travellers on a tight budget. While YMCA and YWCA in Hong Kong are more like four- or three-star hotels, youth hostels offer basic accommodations that are usually located in fairly remote areas, mainly in the New Territories and the outlying islands, but in scenic locations close to outdoor activities and hiking trails – ideal for young adrenaline junkies seeking adventure holidays. Accommodation is based on dormitory or shared-room style with communal facilities, providing an opportunity to make new friends (www.yha.org.hk). Look out for places with a Quality Tourism Services (QTS) visitor accommodation scheme sign, set up by HKTB as a guide to help budget travellers to find reliable accommodation. All the guesthouses and hostels listed are vetted by HKTB on a yearly basis.

Hong Kong Hotels Association has two Hotel Reservation Centre counters at the airport: in the Buffer Halls A & B Arrival Level Terminal 1. For more information, visit www.hkha.org or e-mail: info@hkha.org

Eating Out

Restaurants are usually very busy at lunch time (12:00–14:00), at night and at weekends. Reservation is advisable especially in upscale restaurants. In Chinese restaurants, waiters usually automatically serve Chinese tea, condiments and snacks (such as peanuts and pickles) which could be added to your bill. It is deemed unlucky to stand your chopsticks upright in a bowl of rice as it symbolizes an offering to the dead. When you are served Chinese tea, it is customary to tap your fingers on the table as a 'thank you' gesture. Dress code in restaurants is usually casual, but some may require more formal attire, so check when making a reservation. It is advisable to wear a light shawl or jacket as the air conditioning in some eateries tends to be quite chilly. Beware of eating from street-food carts as some are not licensed and food is often prepared in unhygienic conditions, especially without running water to wash the plates and utensils. Only dine in established hawkers' stalls with proper cooking and washing facilities.

Transport

Hong Kong, as a major hub for air and sea travel, is well served by many international airlines and cruise liners.

Hong Kong International Airport has two terminals with shopping and dining outlets, Internet access, banks, post office, a bureau de change, nursing rooms and playrooms for children, hair and beauty salons, a massage service, as well as entertainment and more facilities. It has an excellent transportation network linking the airport to the city. The Arrival Hall in Terminal 1 has direct access to a variety of transport links including the Airport Express train, buses, tour coaches, hotel transport and taxis to the city.

Taxis: Since most taxi drivers do not speak English, it is advisable to take a card with details of your accommodation in Chinese with you before you leave your hotel to go sightseeing or shopping. Urban taxis are red and those in New Territories are green, while those on Lantau Island are blue. There are extra charges for tunnel and bridge tolls and luggage handling. Always ask for a receipt in case you need to track down the taxi driver or items you may have left in the taxi. It is compulsory by law for passengers to wear seat belts in all motor vehicles.

Airport Express Train: The most efficient way to travel to and from the city is by the Airport Express Train which only takes 24 minutes and travels at 12-minute intervals. The service is in operation from 05:50–01:15 daily, the last train leaving the Airport Station at 00:48. Passengers can have free check-in at Kowloon and Hong Kong stations for selected airlines (check with your individual airlines) from 90 minutes before departure to a day in advance. At Airport Express Hong Kong Station and Kowloon Station there are free bus shuttles to most major hotels with free porter service. Train tickets can be purchased at the airport counters.

CONVERSION CHART

FROM	TO	MULTIPLY BY
Millimetres	Inches	0.0394
Centimetres	Inches	0.3937
Metres	Yards	1.0936
Metres	Feet	3.281
Kilometres	Miles	0.6214
Square kilometres	Square miles	0.386
Hectares	Acres	2.471
Litres	Pints	1.760
Kilograms	Pounds	2.205
Tonnes	Tons	0.984

To convert Celsius to Fahrenheit: x 9 ÷ 5 + 32

Octopus Card: This electronic fare card is excellent for paying for transportation and is accepted by almost all public transport. Many restaurants and shops also accept the Octopus Card as a cash card. They can be purchased and topped up at any MTR stations and at 7-Eleven shops. A refundable deposit of HK$50 is required and any unused value will be refunded within three months. For further details, call Octopus Customer Hotline, tel: 852 2266 2222, or Lost Cards Hotline, tel: 852 2266 2266.

Mass Transit Railway (MTR): Built in 1979 and merged with Kowloon Canton Railway (KCR) in 2007, it is one of the most efficient and extensive railway networks in Asia. It covers Hong Kong from the heart of Central and Causeway Bay to the New Territories and Lantau Island. The 168.1km (104.5 miles) of tracks call at 80 stations on nine lines. In addition, there are the Airport Express Line (with a rapid link to the city) and Light Rail network calling at 68 stations in the northwestern New Territories as feeder service for the MTR and bus services. Most stations have facilities for disabled passengers. MTR stations are located near main shopping centres and tourist attractions. **MTR Hotline,** tel: 852 2881 8888, www.mtr.com.hk

Ferry Services: Hong Kong Island, Kowloon and HKIA are well served by efficient high-speed ferries linking to neighbouring ports in China. Passengers can transit into or out of the Pearl River Delta region via SkyPier in HKIA without the need to pass through HK Customs and Immigration formalities. There are three main ferry companies serving Hong Kong, namely **Turbo Jet** (www.turbojet.com.hk) to Macau and Shenzhen; **Chu Kong Passenger Transport** (CKS) (www.cksp.com.hk) to ports in the Guangdong provinces; **New World First Ferry** (www.nwff.com.hk) to Macau. Terminals are at Macau Ferry Terminal, 202 Connaught Road Central, (MTR Sheung Wan station Exit D), Central. China Ferry Terminal, 33 Canton Road (MTR Tsim Sha Tsui station Exit A1), Kowloon.

Disabled Travellers: Many tourist attractions and public places are user-friendly for disabled visitors. Facilities are available for wheelchair-bound travellers. For peace of mind when planning a trip out, contact the **Social Welfare Department** (www.cyberable.net) for information on public transport or **Transport Dept Services for the Disabled** (www.td.gov.hk) which provides a downloadable handy guide to public transport.

Discount Rail Passes

Airport Express Tourist Pass: An Octopus Card, ideal for travellers arriving at HKIA, with one or two single journeys on the Airport Express Line plus a three-day unlimited ride on the MTR (except Airport Express, Light Rail, MTR Bus, East Rail Line First Class,

Lo Wu and Lok Ma Chau stations). One journey: HK$220; two journeys: HK$300.

Tourist Day Pass: Unlimited one-day travel on MTR (except Airport Express, Light Rail, MTR Bus, East Rail Line First Class and Lo Wu and Lok Ma Chau stations). HK$55.

Disneyland® Resort Line Day Pass: Unlimited one-day travel on MTR to and from Disneyland® Resort station (except Airport Express, Light Rail, MTR Bus and East Rail Line First Class). HK$50.

Time Difference

Hong Kong is GMT + 8.

Weights and Measures

Hong Kong uses the metric system.

General Business Hours

Businesses are generally open Mon–Fri 09:00–17:00, Sat 09:00–13:00, closed Sun and public holidays. Banks are open from 09:00–16:30 Mon–Fri, 09:00–12:30 Sat.

Money Matters

Credit Cards: All major credit cards are accepted in hotels, restaurants and retail and commercial outlets.

Currency: The official currency is the Hong Kong Dollar, subdivided into 100 cents. Notes come in denominations of HK$1000, HK$500, HK$100, HK$50, HK$20 and HK$10. Coins are 10 cents, 20 cents, 50 cents, HK$1, HK2, HK$5 and HK$10. Foreign currencies and traveller's cheques can be exchanged at banks, major post offices, hotels and bureaux de change (note that commission may be charged in some outlets).

Tipping: Service charge of 10% is usually added to restaurant bills. Small tips may be given to taxi drivers, bell-boys, doormen and washroom attendants at your discretion.

Electricity

In Hong Kong electricity is 220 volts, 50HZ. Most hotels provide adaptors.

What to Pack

Hong Kong has a subtropical climate with mild winter and very hot and humid summer. For the cooler season, a light jacket, cardigan or shawl is sufficient, while natural fibre clothing is more comfortable for the hotter season. Wear loose and light coloured apparel during the day time to keep cool. It is useful to pack a foldable umbrella or hat to shelter from the rain and strong sun. A liberal application of high-factor sun block lotion will prevent sunburn when venturing out in the hot sun. Wear comfortable shoes (such as trainers or sandals) for sightseeing. Always carry bottled water when out sightseeing and drink plenty of water to prevent dehydration. Carry loose change for tips. Always ask permission before taking pictures of people. When visiting places of worship, be respectful and dress appropriately. Shoes may have to be removed before entering certain temples (observe the locals).

Language

The official languages are English and Chinese. Cantonese is spoken by 95% of the population, though Mandarin (Putonghua) has become more commonly spoken since the handover. English is widely spoken in commercial outfits, shops, hotels and in the tourist industry but not among the older generation and in rural areas. All signage and street names are bilingual in both Chinese and English. Chinese is a tonal language and each tone of the same word can mean a different thing. It could be tricky when spoken but have a go anyway. It pleases and amuses the locals when foreigners make an effort to speak the local lingo.

USEFUL CANTONESE PHRASES

Hello • *Lei hou mah*
Good morning • *Jou san*
Good night • *Jou tau*
Good bye • *Bai Bai*
Good • *Hou hou*
Thank you • *Um goi*
Yes • *Hai*
No • *Um Hai*
How much is this? • *Lee goh sai doh chin aah?*
Where is the toilet? • *Chiso hai bin doh aah?*
I don't speak Cantonese • *Ngoh umsik gong gwongdungwa*
Bon Appetite • *Sik Fan*
Do you have an English menu? • *Neih deih yau mah yingman chaanpai aah?*
Tea • *cha*
Coffee • *Gah fei*
Milk • *Ngow Nai*
Bread • *Meen bao*
Beer • *Beh Jow*
Water • *Sui*
Can I have the bill please? • *Um goi mai dan?*
Take me to the hotel • *Ching leng ngoh doh ngoh ge jai deem*
Train • *Foh Chay*
Taxi • *teksi*
Bus • *Bah See*
Doctor • *Yee seng*
Pharmacy • *Yeurk Fong*

Health

Government water supply exceeds World Health Organisation standards but it is advisable to drink bottled water. Hong Kong imposes strict health laws and littering carries a fine of HK$1500. Smoking is prohibited in most indoor areas including restaurants, malls and bars.

Smoking is also banned at some outdoor areas such as public beaches and swimming pools, transport interchanges and outdoor escalators.

Hong Kong has a comprehensive health care service in efficiently run hospitals. Visitors using their Accident and Emergency Service are charged a set fee of HK$570 per visit (treatment will still be administered even if a visitor cannot pay the fee at the time of visit). Details of health services can be found on the Hospital Authority website, www.ha.org.hk

Safety

Hong Kong is generally very safe by day or night. Streets are frequently patrolled by policemen. Nevertheless, use your own judgement and exercise caution by storing valuable items in a hotel safe. Beware of pickpockets in crowded places, avoid being conned by street touts with cheap offers, and stay in well-lit main streets and thoroughfares at night as a precaution. Report any loss of property to your hotel or police station (especially for an insurance claim). It is advisable to keep photocopies of credit cards and passports at home and also to take a copy on your travels for your record in case they are stolen. It will expedite replacement if you have the details at hand.

Shopping Tips

Prices in major shopping malls and departmental stores are always clearly displayed and fixed. Smaller retail outlets and street markets do not usually display prices and bargaining is encouraged. HKTB has warned against street touts and traders and they advise tourists not to follow them to any warehouses or showrooms nor buy any counterfeit or pirated goods. Check your receipts and ensure that all details and verbal agreements are fully listed. If buying electrical goods, make sure they are compatible in your home country and that they carry a guarantee. For ease of mind, look out for shops and restaurants that have been vetted by HKTB displaying the sign QTS (Quality Tourism Services).

Consumer Assistance: In case of dispute or for further information, contact the Consumer Council Hotline, tel: 852 2929 2222. Their operating hours are Mon–Fri 09:00–17:30.

Useful Numbers

Emergency Services:
Police, Fire & Ambulance: 999
Police Hotline: 852 2527 7177
Others:
Hong Kong International Airport: 852 2181 8888
Directory Enquiries: 1081
Overseas IDD & Cardphone Enquiries: 10013.
Hong Kong Country code: 852
Weather Forecast (Hong Kong Observatory): 1878 200
Immigration Dept (24 hours): 852 2824 6111
Department of Health: 852 2961 8989
Consumer Council Hotline (shopping and consumer rights): 852 2929 2222

Communications

Hong Kong is wired up to the latest technology providing a sophisticated and efficient telecommunication system. Local calls on private landlines are free and public telephones charge HK$1 for five minutes. Hotels usually charge for calls. Mobile/cell phones are convenient for visitors as Hong Kong is hooked up with most wireless systems around the world (e.g. GSM900; PCS1800; CDMA and WCDMA). Check with your service provider for roaming facilities before leaving home. Local SIM cards or mobile phones can be rented (check with 7-Eleven shops or telecommunication shops). There are free Wi-Fi services at HKIA terminals 1 and 2. Some public places such as cafés and MTR stations offer free Internet terminals. Most hotels provide broadband Internet access (check with individual hotels for terms and charges).

GOOD READING

Martin Booth (2005) *Gweilo: A Memoir of a Hong Kong Childhood*. Bantam Press.
Timothy Mo (2000) *The Monkey King*. Paddleless Press.
James O'Reilly, Larry Habegger and Sean O'Reilly (editors) (2000) *Hong Kong*. Travelers' Tales.
Han Suyin (1972) *A Many Splendoured Thing*. Triad Books.
Steve Tsang (2007) *A Modern History of Hong Kong*. I. B. Tauris.

INDEX

Note: Numbers in **bold** indicate photographs